WISDOM LITERATURE
IN MESOPOTAMIA AND ISRAEL

D1344497

Society of Biblical Literature

Symposium Series

Christopher R. Matthews, Editor

Number 36

WISDOM LITERATURE
IN MESOPOTAMIA AND ISRAEL
edited by
Richard J. Clifford

WISDOM LITERATURE
IN MESOPOTAMIA AND ISRAEL

edited by
Richard J. Clifford

Society of Biblical Literature
Atlanta

WISDOM LITERATURE
IN MESOPOTAMIA AND ISRAEL

Copyright © 2007 by the Society of Biblical Literature

Library of Congress Cataloging-in-Publication Data

Wisdom literature in Mesopotamia and Israel / edited by Richard J. Clifford.
    p. cm. — (Society of Biblical Literature symposium series ; no. 36)
    Includes index.
    ISBN 978-1-58983-219-0 (paper binding : alk. paper)
    1. Wisdom literature—Criticism, interpretation, etc. 2. Assyro-Babylonian literature—History and criticism. I. Clifford, Richard J.

BS1455.W563 2007a
223'.06—dc22

                2007024579

14 13 12 11 10 09 08 07   5 4 3 2 1

Printed in the United States of America on acid-free, recycled paper conforming to ANSI/NISO Z39.48-1992 (R1997) and ISO 9706:1994 standards for paper permanence.

TABLE OF CONTENTS

Abbreviations vii

Introduction
Richard J. Clifford xi

PART ONE: THE CONTEXT OF WISDOM IN MESOPOTAMIA

1. The Social and Intellectual Setting of Babylonian Wisdom Literature
   Paul-Alain Beaulieu 3

2. Why Wisdom Became a Secret: On Wisdom as a Written Genre
   Karel van der Toorn 21

PART TWO: STUDIES IN BABYLONIAN WISDOM TEXTS

3. An Allusion to the Šamaš Hymn in The Dialogue of Pessimism
   Victor Avigdor Hurowitz 33

4. The Wisdom of Šūpê-amēlī—A Deathbed Debate between
   a Father and Son
   Victor Avigdor Hurowitz 37

PART THREE: COMPARISONS OF MESOPOTAMIAN AND
BIBLICAL TEXTS AND MOTIFS

5. Sages with a Sense of Humor: The Babylonian Dialogue
   between the Master and His Servant and the Book of Qoheleth
   Edward L. Greenstein 55

6. Cosmos, Temple, House: Building and Wisdom in
 Mesopotamia and Israel
 Raymond C. Van Leeuwen 67

PART FOUR: BIBLICAL WISDOM LITERATURE

7. Beginnings, Endings, and Life's Necessities in Biblical Wisdom
 James L. Crenshaw 93

Contributors 107

Index of Ancient Documents 109

Index of Modern Authors Cited 113

ABBREVIATIONS

AB	Anchor Bible
ABL	*Assyrian and Babylonian Letters Belonging to the Kouyunjik Collections of the British Museum.* Edited by R. F. Harper. 14 vols. Chicago, 1892–1914.
ABRL	Anchor Bible Reference Library
AfO	*Archiv für Orientforschung*
AfOB	Archiv für Orientforschung: Beiheft
AHw	*Akkadisches Handwörterbuch.* W. von Soden. 3 vols. Wiesbaden, 1965–81
ANEP	*The Ancient Near East in Pictures Relating to the Old Testament.* Edited by J. B. Pritchard. 2nd ed. Princeton, 1969
ANET	*Ancient Near Eastern Texts Relating to the Old Testament.* Edited by J. B. Pritchard; 3rd ed. Princeton, 1969
AnBib	Analecta biblica
AnOr	Analecta Orientalia
AnSt	*Anatolian Studies*
AOAT	Alter Orient und Altes Testament
AOS	American Oriental Series
ARAB	*Ancient Records of Assyria and Babylonia.* Daniel David Luckenbill. 2 vols. Chicago, 1926–1927
ARI	*Assyrian Royal Inscriptions.* A. K. Grayson. 2 vols. Records of the Ancient Near East. Wiesbaden, 1972–1976.
ATD	Altes Testament Deutsch
AuOr	*Aula Orientalis*
AuOrSup	Aula Orientalis Supplementa
BASOR	*Bulletin of the American Schools of Oriental Research*
BETL	Bibliotheca ephemeridum theologicarum lovaniensium
BK	Biblischer Kommentar
BN	*Biblische Notizen*

BWL	*Babylonian Wisdom Literature.* W. G. Lambert. Oxford, 1960
BZAW	Beihefte zur Zeitschrift für die alttestamentliche Wissenschaft
BZNW	Beihefte zur Zeitschrift für die neutestamentliche Wissenschaft
CAD	*The Assyrian Dictionary of the Oriental Institute of the University of Chicago.* Chicago, 1956-
CBQ	*Catholic Biblical Quarterly*
CBQMS	Catholic Biblical Quarterly Monograph Series
COS	*The Context of Scripture.* Edited by W. W. Hall. 3 vols. Leiden, 1997–2002
CRRAI	Comptes rendus, Rencontre Assyriologique Internationale
CTJ	*Calvin Theological Journal*
DDD	*Dictionary of Deities and Demons in the Bible.* 2nd ed. Edited by K. van der Toorn, B. Becking, and P. W. van der Horst. Leiden, 1999
ETCSL	Electronic Text Corpus of Sumerian Literature (http://www-etcsl. orient. ox. ac. uk/)
FAT	Forschungen zum Alten Testament
FOTL	Forms of Old the Testament Literature
HALOT	Koehler, L, W. Baumgartner, and J. J. Stamm, *The Hebrew and Aramaic Lexicon of the Old Testament.* Translated and edited under the supervision of M. E. J. Richardson. 4 vols. Leiden, 1994–1999
HAT	Handbuch zum Alten Testament
HBT	*Horizons in Biblical Theology*
ICC	International Critical Commentary
IOS	Israel Oriental Studies
JANESCU	*Journal of the Ancient Near Eastern Society of Columbia University*
JAOS	*Journal of the American Oriental Society*
JBL	*Journal of Biblical Literature*
JCS	*Journal of Cuneiform Studies*
JQR	*Jewish Quarterly Review*
JQRSupp	Jewish Quarterly Review: Supplement Series
JSOT	*Journal for the Study of the Old Testament*
JSOTSup	Journal for the Study of the Old Testament: Supplement Series
KTU	*Die keilalphabetischen Texte aus Ugarit.* Edited by M. Dietrich, O. Loretz, and J. Sanmartín. AOAT 24/1.

Neukirchen-Vluyn,1976. 2d enlarged ed. of *KTU*: *The Cuneiform Texts from Ugarit, Ras Ibn Hani, and Other Places.* Edited by M. Dietrich, O. Loretz, and J. Sanmartín. Münster, 1995 (= *CTU*)

LCL	Loeb Classical Library
MDAI	Mitteilungen des deutschen archäologischen Instituts
MSL	*Materialen zum sumerischen Lexikon.* Benno Landsberger, ed.
MVAG	Mitteilungen der Vorderasiatisch-ägyptischen Gesellschaft. Vols. 1–44. 1896–1939
NCBC	New Century Bible Commentary
NIB	*New Interpreter's Bible*
OBO	Orbis biblicus et orientalis
OIP	Oriental Institute Publications
OLA	Orientalia lovaniensia analecta
OLP	Orientalia lovaniensia periodica
Or	*Orientalia* (NS)
OTL	Old Testament Library
OTP	*Old Testament Pseudepigrapha.* Edited by J. H. Charlesworth. 2 vols. New York, 1983
RA	*Revue d'assyriologie et archéologie orientale*
RIMB	Royal Inscriptions of Mesopotamia, Babylonian Period
RlA	*Reallexikon der Assyriologie.* Edited by Erich Ebeling et al. Berlin, 1928-
SAA	State Archives of Assyria
SAAS	State Archives of Assyria Studies
SAACT	State Archives of Assyria Cuneiform Texts
SB	Sources Bibliques
SBLDS	Society of Biblical Literature Dissertation Series
SBLWAW	Society of Biblical Literature Writings from the Ancient World
SBS	Stuttgarter Bibelstudien
SHR	Studies in the History of Religions (supplement to *Numen*)
SVT	Supplements to *Vetus Testamentum*
TLOT	*Theological Lexicon of the Old Testament.* Edited by E. Jenni with assistance from C. Westermann. Translated by M. E. Biddle. 3 vols. Peabody, Mass, 1997
TUAT	*Texte aus der Umwelt des Alten Testaments.* Edited by Otto Kaiser. Gütersloh,1984–
TZ	*Theologische Zeitschrift*
UF	*Ugarit-Forschungen*

UVB	Uruk-Warka Vorläufiger Bericht
VT	*Vetus Testamentum*
VTSup	Supplements to Vetus Testamentum
WBC	Word Biblical Commentary
ZA	*Zeitschrift für Assyriologie*
ZAW	*Zeitschrift für die alttestamentaliche Wissenschaft*

INTRODUCTION

Richard J. Clifford

This volume in the SBL Symposium series grew out of a panel on "Mesopotamian Wisdom Literature and Its Legacy in the Ancient Near East" at the annual meeting of the Society of Biblical Literature in 2004 at San Antonio, Texas. Panelists Paul-Alain Beaulieu, Karel van der Toorn, Peter Machinist, and Victor Avigdor Hurowitz—biblical scholars as well as distinguished Assyriologists—gave papers on Mesopotamian wisdom literature. The editor of this volume, Richard Clifford, was chair of the SBL panel. Though primarily concerned with Mesopotamia, the panelists adduced parallels to other cultures and literatures, including ancient Israel. One paper was on the intellectual and social setting of Babylonian wisdom literature; another was on the development of the concept of wisdom especially in the Old Babylonian and Standard Versions of the Gilgamesh Epic. Two papers were fresh studies of important though difficult wisdom texts, one long known and the other recently published. So well attended was the meeting and so stimulating the discussion that the panelists and chair decided to publish the papers and invite other scholars to contribute to the volume. The result is before you. Since all the papers focus on specific issues or texts, a general guide to the publication of Mesopotamian wisdom literature in its relationship to biblical literature is called for.

THE WISDOM TEXTS OF MESOPOTAMIA

In his perceptive essay "Foreign Semitic Influence on the Wisdom of Israel and Its Appropriation in the Book of Proverbs,"[1] John Day notes that biblical scholars have generally been more attentive to the influence of Egyptian literature than they have to the influence of Semitic literature. This is especially true for Proverbs with its wicked–righteous contrasts, graded numerical proverbs, centrality of fear of the Lord, and personification of wisdom, but *mutatis mutandis* it is true of other wisdom books as well. One reason, perhaps, is that the literature of Mesopotamia, until recently, has

---

1. *Wisdom in Ancient Israel: Essays in Honour of J. A. Emerton* (ed. John Day et al.; Cambridge: Cambridge University Press, 1995), 55–70.

been not so well published and accessible as the Egyptian material. Yet the Mesopotamian wisdom literature is a finite corpus of texts and is reasonably well understood, though problems of interpretation are many.

W. G. Lambert's magisterial *Babylonian Wisdom Literature,* published in 1960,[2] marks a watershed in the study of "wisdom literature" from Mesopotamia. Lambert established the relevant Akkadian texts and provided them with introductions, translations, and notes; his choices and his titles have been extremely influential. Here is a list of the major works he selected: The Poem of the Righteous Sufferer (*Ludlul bēl nēmeqi*), The Babylonian Theodicy, Precepts and Admonitions (Instructions of Shuruppak, Counsels of Wisdom, Counsels of a Pessimist, Advice to a Prince), Preceptive Hymns (a bilingual Hymn to Ninurta, The Shamash Hymn), The Dialogue of Pessimism, Fables or Contest Literature (The Tamarisk and the Palm, The Fable of the Willow, Nisaba and Wheat, The Ox and the Horse, The Fable of the Fox, and The Fable of the Riding-donkey), Several Popular Sayings, and Proverbs (bilingual and Babylonian). Lambert's influence can be seen in Dietz Otto Edzard's survey of Sumerian literature in *RlA*.[3] Accepting Lambert's judgment that "'Wisdom' is strictly a misnomer as applied to Babylonian literature," his list is somewhat restrictive: fables, riddles, and collections of proverbs. Commenting on Akkadian literature in the same article, Wolfgang Röllig agrees with Edzard that "wisdom literature" is not a distinct genre, though his group is larger than Edzard's: narratives with a didactic thrust (he includes *Enūma elish*), didactic works (Instructions of Shuruppak, Counsels of Wisdom, and Counsels of a Pessimist), hymns with a didactic tone (Hymn to Ninurta, Shamash Hymn), The Babylonian Theodicy, collections of proverbs (bilingual or Babylonian), and several fables.[4]

Links between Mesopotamian and biblical literature have long been recognized— think of the Babel–Bibel controversy and the early recognition of a connection between The Babylonian Theodicy and Job. More searching comparisons of the wisdom material have had to wait for more texts and better editions. The first edition (1909) of *Altorientalische Texte zum Alten Testament* (ed. Hugo Gressmann; 2d ed.; Berlin: de Gruyter, 1926) had no separate sections for "wisdom" and contained little relevant material in other sections. The second edition in 1926, however, introduced a special section "Weltanschauung und Weisheit" and translated what was then known of The Dialogue of Pessimism, The Babylonian Theodicy, some proverbs, and the Fable of the Tamarisk and the Psalm. The English successor of *Altorientalische Texte zum Alten Testament, Ancient Near Eastern Texts Relating to the Old Testament* (3d ed.; Princeton: Princeton University Press, 1969), in its third edition devoted one of its ten sections to "Didactic and Wisdom Literature"; it contains most of W. G. Lambert's choices.

---

2. *Babylonian Wisdom Literature* (Oxford: Clarendon, 1960), 1. Lambert gives a brief update in "Some New Babylonian Wisdom Literature," in Day et al., *Wisdom in Ancient Israel,* 30–42.

3. "Literatur," 7.1–2 (1987): 45–46.

4. "Literatur," 7.1–2 (1987): 59–61.

Anthologies since *ANET* (ed. J. B. Pritchard; 3rd ed.; Princeton: Princeton University Press, 1969) have continued the trend toward more coverage of Mesopotamian wisdom literature. *Texte aus der Umwelt des Alten Testaments* devoted an entire volume to Sumerian and Akkadian *Weisheitstexte* (*TUAT* 3; ed. Willem H. Ph. Römer and Wolfram von Soden; Gütersloh: Gerd Mohn, 1990), though its 188 pages make no claim to complete coverage of the extant texts. Of the Sumerian material, Willem H. Ph. Römer edited selections from five of the twenty-seven extant collections of proverbs, five disputes, four riddles, two examples of "narrative-didactic literature" (Praise of the Scribal Art, Instructions of Shuruppak), two satires (Son of the Tablet House, The Father and His Useless Son), two school dialogues, and an excursus on "A Man and His God." Wolfram von Soden was responsible for the Akkadian material: The Praise of the Righteous Sufferer (*Ludlul bēl nēmeqi*), A Man and His God, Lament of a Sufferer with a Prayer to Marduk, The Babylonian Theodicy, The Dialogue of Pessimism, Counsels of Wisdom, Counsels of a Pessimist, Advice to a Prince, The Poor Man of Nippur,[5] and three fables. *The Context of Scripture: Canonical Compositions from the Biblical World* (ed. W. W. Hallo; 3 vols.; Leiden: Brill, 1997–2002) frames Mesopotamian wisdom literature with the heading "individual focus" and includes the main compositions treated by Lambert.

Two more anthologies of Mesopotamian wisdom texts should be mentioned, though the texts were not primarily selected for their relevance to the Bible. Both anthologies are very ably edited. The Electronic Text Corpus of Sumerian Literature (ETCSL) is an Internet site containing transliterations and translations of all available Sumerian compositions.[6] Among its many headings, "Wisdom Literature" is in quotation marks to indicate that the term is being used broadly; the heading includes transliterations and translations of Instructions of Shuruppak, The Farmer's Instruction, and The Three Ox-Drivers from Adab. Debate Poems, Dialogues and Diatribes, Proverb Collections, and Other Proverbs are all listed under separate headings. It is clear that "wisdom literature" is not a major category in the Electronic Corpus. An indispensable source of Mesopotamian texts, including wisdom texts, is Benjamin R. Foster, *Before the Muses: An Anthology of Akkadian Literature* (3d ed.; Bethesda, Md.: CDL Press, 2005). The third edition is one hundred pages longer than the previous edition and has been updated.[7]

---

5. See the important treatment of J. S. Cooper in *JCS* 27 (1975) 164–74.

6. ETCSL should be cited as J. A. Black, G. Cunningham, J. Ebeling, E. Flückiger-Hawker, E. Robson, J. Taylor, and G. Zólyomi, *The Electronic Text Corpus of Sumerian Literature* (http://etcsl.orinst.ox.ac.uk/), Oxford, 1998–.

7. A concise guide to Wisdom texts from Mesopotamia and Egypt is Kenton L. Sparks, *Ancient Texts for the Study of the Hebrew Bible: A Guide to the Background Literature* (Peabody, Mass.: Hendrickson, 2005), 56–83.

PART ONE

The Context of Wisdom in Mesopotamia

The Social and Intellectual Setting of Babylonian Wisdom Literature

Paul-Alain Beaulieu

Ancient Mesopotamia produced a substantial corpus of texts that can be subsumed under the label of wisdom literature.[1] This label was originally borrowed from biblical scholarship, and the definition of the Mesopotamian corpus of wisdom still largely depends on parallels that can be established with biblical literature. Thus, Mesopotamian collections of proverbs and moral precepts, instructions, reflections on the problem of theodicy, and laments of the pious sufferer have all been readily included in the category of wisdom because they find a reflection in the Bible. To this list have been added such genres as fables and disputations, which are less well attested in Hebrew literature but undeniably belong to the same stream of philosophical reflection that is deemed characteristic of wisdom literature. The general tenor of wisdom texts is to teach the art of leading a successful life, in harmony with society and the divine will. There is a general sense that most of Mesopotamian and Egyptian wisdom literature originated in learned and official circles and served to reinforce the sense of loyalty to the established order, while at the same time encouraging blind faith in the gods, especially in times of trial and adversity. The locus of origin of biblical wisdom literature in a courtly environment is debatable, given its largely postexilic setting. Nonetheless, its high literary content points at least to an intellectual milieu, perhaps in some cases one close to official circles.

Wisdom literature is such a vast and inclusive notion that scholars have always experienced great difficulties in clearly defining its boundaries. Indeed, it is largely an intuitive category, based on a general recognition of certain themes and questions that wisdom literature is expected to address. Problems arise when we consider ancient classifications of that literature. In ancient Mesopotamia, there was no such concept or category as wisdom literature. In Sumerian, the word for wisdom is nam-kù-zu, which can be translated literally as "pure, sacred knowledge." Its Akkadian equivalent *nēmequ* appears in the incipit of the most famous work of Babylonian wisdom literature, *Ludlul bēl nēmeqi*, "Let me praise the Lord of Wisdom," composed probably at

---

1. The main study is Lambert, *BWL*.

the end of the second millennium B.C.E. The Lord of Wisdom is the god Marduk, and as it turns out the words for wisdom, nam-kù-zu and *nēmequ*, are most consistently associated with Marduk and his father Ea, (Enki in Sumerian), in Mesopotamian religious and scholarly literature. Because these two words refer occasionally to general notions of knowledge and wisdom, they overlap semantically in part with the Hebrew word חכמה and also with Greek σοφία. In their primary meaning, however, they really describe a specific skill such as a craft, and by extension all the skills and knowledge necessary to civilized life. The word חכמה occasionally conveys the same meaning in Hebrew. In Mesopotamia, the god Ea, in his role as bringer of the arts of civilization to the human race, was the god of wisdom par excellence and the craftsman god. It is notable that the words nam-kù-zu and *nēmequ* occur infrequently in the context of wisdom literature. This contrasts sharply with the Hebrew equivalent חכמה, which appears much more frequently in the wisdom books than in any other parts of the Bible. Indeed, more than half of the biblical attestations of the word חכמה occur in Job, Proverbs, and Ecclesiastes. It also seems a fair assessment to say that one of the purposes of the biblical wisdom books is to praise and propagate חכמה. The Mesopotamian situation is far less clear. We do not find any explicit statement that the aim of Mesopotamian wisdom literature was to teach *nēmequ*. Only one text, the Babylonian Theodicy, composed at the end of the second millennium, appears to engage the subject of wisdom directly. Therefore, we are confronted with two questions. What is the place of wisdom literature in the intellectual and social world of ancient Mesopotamia, and in what manner does it relate to the concepts of nam-kù-zu and *nēmequ*?

Wisdom literature has a long history in Mesopotamia, starting with the Sumerian literary tradition. We know Sumerian literature mostly from school copies made at Nippur and other cities during the Isin-Larsa period. This was the literature taught by master scribes to their pupils in the *edubba*. A portion of this literature consists of proverbs, fables, disputations, instructions, and dialogues, often labeled as "rhetorical collections" or "scribal training literature" by scholars. The most significant piece of wisdom literature in Sumerian is the Instructions of Shuruppak.[2] Its great antiquity and popularity is evidenced by the large number of manuscripts of it that have survived. These include, among others, an early version found at Abu Salabikh, dating to approximately 2500 B.C.E., as well as a fragment from Adab from approximately 2400 B.C.E. There are also two fragments of an Akkadian version, one dating to the fifteenth century, the other one to the end of the second millennium. The Instructions of Shuruppak consist of counsels and proverbs addressed by Shuruppak, son of Ubartutu, to his son Ziusudra. The name Shuruppak is identical with that of the city of Shuruppak. The city of Shuruppak ranks as one of the five antediluvian cities in the Mesopotamian tradition, alongside Eridu, Bad-Tibira, Larak, and Sippar. Therefore,

---

2. Bendt Alster, *The Instructions of Shuruppak: A Sumerian Proverb Collection* (Mesopotamia 2; Copenhagen: Akademisk Forlag, 1974).

it is not surprising that the classical version of the Instructions taught in Old Babylonian schools sets the teachings of Shuruppak in primeval time, as expressed by its
initial verse: "In those days, in those far remote days." The son of Shuruppak, Ziusudra, was the Mesopotamian Noah according to the Sumerian Flood Story, also called
the Eridu Genesis.[3] Ziusudra appears again as teacher of wisdom in the Sumerian tale
of the Death of Gilgamesh.[4] This composition tells us that Gilgamesh, having accom-
plished all his exploits and reached the abode of Ziusudra, received from him the revelation of the rites of Sumer, which he brought back to Uruk in order to restart
civilization after the flood.[5]

Ziusudra resurfaces in the same role in the Standard Babylonian version of the
Epic of Gilgamesh, this time under his Akkadian name, Utnapishtim.[6] According to
the opening verses of the epic, Gilgamesh undertook his journey on a quest for wisdom and antediluvian knowledge: "He (Gilgamesh) [learned] the totality of wisdom
(nēmequ) about everything. He saw the secret and uncovered the hidden, he brought
back a message from the antediluvian age."[7] Having reached the edge of the world, he
encountered Utnapishtim, who told him the story of the flood and his own miracu-
lous survival (tablet XI). He also imparted the secret of immortality to Gilgamesh,
who in the end failed to gain it and returned to Uruk wiser but empty handed. We
encounter Ziusudra again in the third century B.C.E. in the Greek writings of the
Babylonian cleric Berossus, this time under the name Xisouthros. Berossus's account
of the flood closely follows earlier traditions but specifies that antediluvian knowledge was transmitted in written, not oral, form. Before the flood, the god Kronos
(= Ea) ordered Xisouthros to collect all writings and bury them in Sippar. After the
flood, the buried tablets were turned over to humankind in order to start civilization
again and renew Babylonia.[8] Finally, it is possible that Shuruppak and Ziusudra appear
in a garbled form in an Akkadian wisdom text found at Ugarit that claims to contain
instructions of Šupê-awilum (= Shuruppak?) to his son Zuranku (= Ziusudra?), a

---

3. Thorkild Jacobsen, "The Eridu Genesis," *JBL* 100 (1981): 513–29.

4. This composition is now better known with the publication of new manuscripts from Meturan
(modern Tell Haddad) by Antoine Cavigneaux and Farouk N. H. Al-Rawi, *Gilgameš et la mort: Textes de
Tell Haddad VI* (Cuneiform Monographs 19; Groningen: Styx Publications, 2000). English translation by
Andrew R. George, *The Epic of Gilgamesh: A New Translation* (New York: Barnes & Noble Books, 1999),
195–208.

5. This is clearly expressed in lines 148–50: "You reached [Ziusudra in his abode! The rites of Sumer],
forgotten since distant days of old, [the rituals and customs—you] brought them down to the land." See
George, *Epic of Gilgamesh*, 202, and Cavigneaux and Al-Rawi, *Gilgameš et la mort*, 30–31 (Sumerian text)
and 56 (translation).

6. All previous editions and translations are now superseded by Andrew R. George, *The Babylonian
Gilgamesh Epic: Introduction, Critical Edition and Cuneiform Texts* (2 vols.; Oxford: Oxford University Press,
2003).

7. George, *Babylonian Gilgamesh Epic*, 538–39.

8. Gerald P. Verbrugghe and John M. Wickersham, *Berossos and Manetho, Introduced and Translated:
Native Traditions in Ancient Mesopotamia and Egypt* (Ann Arbor: University of Michigan Press, 1996), 49–
50.

wisdom comparable to that of Enlilbanda ("Junior Enlil"), another name for the god Ea, the source of all wisdom.[9]

The tradition about Ziusudra plays an important role in the sapiential tradition of ancient Mesopotamia. It also tells us something important about the purpose of wisdom teachings: they were foundational to civilized life. More particularly, the Ziusudra tradition puts much weight on the connection between wisdom, kingship, and antediluvian knowledge. The same themes appear in the Instructions of Ur-Ninurta, a Sumerian composition in praise of King Ur-Ninurta of the First Dynasty of Isin, who reigned at the end of the twentieth century B.C.E.[10] These instructions portray Ur-Ninurta mythically as reestablisher of order, justice, and cultic practices in his country after the flood, therefore as an emulator of Gilgamesh and Ziusudra, two figures who were clearly pivotal in the propagation of the royal ideology. Mesopotamian tradition viewed Ziusudra as the last king before the flood and, therefore, as the last in a long line of culture bringers, both gods and mythical beings, who created civilization in Sumer. His role was to ensure the continuation of civilization after the flood by teaching its essential elements to the survivors. This underlies his relation to Gilgamesh. Gilgamesh embodied the archetype of the postdiluvian ruler who must relearn the components of civilization, the wisdom, in order to guide his subjects on the right path. It appears, therefore, that wisdom was very much linked from earliest times to the mystique of the monarchy, an institution that came down from heaven twice according to the Sumerian King List, once at the beginning of time and on a second occasion after the flood. The king was responsible for the refoundation of the land in historical times on the model of the civilization of the mythical period before the flood. For that purpose he needed to appropriate the wisdom of antediluvian kings. The same notion is expressed in a bilingual inscription of King Nebuchadnezzar I of the Second Dynasty of Isin (reigned 1126–1104 B.C.E.).[11] The king, endowed with perfect wisdom (nam-kù-zu) by the god Marduk, claims to belong to a "distant line of kingship from before the flood" and to be an "offspring of Enmeduranki, king of Sippar." Here Ziusudra is replaced with Enmeduranki, who was the last king before the flood, according to the Uruk List of Rulers and Sages, known from a manuscript dating to the Hellenistic period.[12] In this manner, the scribes of Nebuchadnezzar I

---

9. Translation with notes and references to primary edition and previous commentaries in Benjamin R. Foster, *Before the Muses* (Bethesda, Md.: CDL Press, 1993), 1:332–35.

10. The main edition is by Bendt Alster, "The Instructions of Ur-Ninurta and Related Compositions," *Or* 60 (1991): 141–57, with further notes in his "Corrections to the Instructions of Urninurta and Related Compositions," *Nouvelles assyriologiques brèves et utilitaires* (Paris: S.E.P.O.A., 1992), no. 83. Alster also translates the *Instructions* in *COS* 1.570.

11. Wilfred G. Lambert, "Enmeduranki and Related Matters," *JCS* 21 (1967): 128–31, with additional fragments by the same author in his article "The Seed of Kingship," in *Le palais et la royauté: Archéologie et civilisation* (ed. Paul Garelli; CRRAI XIX; Paris: Geuthner, 1974), 427–40. The text has been republished by Grant Frame, *Rulers of Babylonia: From the Second Dynasty of Isin to the End of Assyrian Domination (1157–612 BC)* (RIMB 2; Toronto: University of Toronto Press, 1995), 23–28.

12. The text was initially edited and discussed by Jacobus van Dijk, "Die Inschriftenfunde," *UVB* (*Vorläufiger Bericht über die Ausgrabungen in Uruk-Warka*) 18 (1962): 44–51 and pl. 27. The autograph copy

ascribed to their ruler the role of refounder of civilization after the flood by means of his privileged connection to the last antediluvian king.

Another important aspect of the Ziusudra tradition is the inherent fluidity of the concept of wisdom. The Instructions of Shuruppak consist simply of advice on proper conduct, and in this respect they bear an evident similarity to the wisdom teachings of Egypt and Israel. Yet, according to the Death of Gilgamesh, the teachings of Ziusudra also included the rites of Sumer (me ki-en-gi-ra-ke₄), that is to say, the arts and crafts of civilized life and the cultic prescriptions essential to a proper worship of the gods. The pristine nature of these rites, the *mes*, is reflected in the names of several antediluvian kings and sages: Enmeduranki means "Lord of the rites of Nippur" (En = "lord"; me = "rites"; duranki = "bond of heaven and the netherworld," a cosmological name for the city of Nippur); similarly, Enmegalanna means "Lord of the great rites of heavens" (gal = "great"; an-na = "of heaven"), and Enmedugga means "Lord of the good/propitious rites" (dug-ga = "good" with genitive). In the Standard Babylonian Epic of Gilgamesh, on the other hand, there is no mention of rites or other prescriptions in the long exchange between Utnapishtim and Gilgamesh. Although the epic clearly defines as wisdom (*nēmequ*) the secret knowledge acquired by Gilgamesh on his journey, it never states explicitly the nature and content of this *nēmequ*. But there is an equally profound lesson in wisdom that Gilgamesh learns from Utnapishtim. Humans cannot attain eternal life. The moral teachings of the epic center on the rejection of hubris, the acceptance of human mortality, and ultimately on the submission to fate and to the order created by the gods. These are major themes addressed by wisdom literature as traditionally defined. In this sense, the epic appears to represent the quintessential sapiential teaching. These themes, however, cannot easily be separated from the larger context of religion and ritual, even though wisdom literature does not always make these connections fully explicit. After all, the prologue of the Standard Babylonian Epic still portrays Gilgamesh as restorer of cult centers and religious rites after the flood, highlighting the traditional role of the king as culture bringer (Tablet I, 43–44). The rites, the *mes*, represent the order willed by the gods in primeval times. Fulfilling ritual prescriptions and serving the gods formed an integral part of wisdom. Every important Mesopotamian text that offers a philosophical reflection on divine abandonment presupposes that failure to accomplish the divine will through neglect of some unknown rite or prescription can be the cause of individual misfortune. The sphere of wisdom extends even to the crafts of the exorcist and diviner, because they too control arts given by the gods to attain that superior knowledge. Indeed, the fame of the antediluvian king Enmeduranki as recipient and giver of wisdom did not rest on his moral teachings but on the fact that he received

---

was later republished by Jacobus van Dijk and Werner R. Mayer, *Texte aus dem Rēš-Heiligtum in Uruk-Warka* (Baghdader Mitteilungen, Beiheft 2; Berlin: Gebr. Mann Verlag, 1980), text 89. The list was subsequently discussed by William W. Hallo, "On the Antiquity of Sumerian Literature," *JAOS* 83 (1963): 174–76, and briefly by various authors since. Line 7 gives the name of the last king before the flood as follows: 7. [*ina tar-ṣi*] ¹*en-me-dur-an-ki* : ¹*ù-tu-abzu* ABGAL "[At the time] of (king) Enmeduranki, Utuabzu was the *apkallu*."

the revelation of the arts of divination from Šamaš and Adad, the two gods of Sippar, in primeval times. The fully integrated nature of wisdom, religion, ritual, and divination becomes more evident as we now consider the important transformations of Babylonian scholarship and religion during the second half of the second millennium.

In the realm of Sumerian wisdom literature, I have thus far mentioned instructions, proverbs, fables, and disputations, but at the beginning of the second millennium we also witness the emergence of the motif of theodicy with the figure of the pious sufferer. This motif represents, so to speak, the darker side of wisdom, its negative mirror image. How can a man who has followed all the teachings of traditional wisdom, who is prudent, obedient, pious, and learned, who has lived in accordance with every ritual prescription, suffer from reversals of fortune without the higher powers, gods and king, being sensitive to his misery? For Israel, this eternal question is masterfully expounded in the Book of Job, which remains indeed the obligatory point of comparison for any similar composition from antiquity.[13] Five such works of literature have come down to us from ancient Mesopotamia. The earliest one is the Sumerian text known as A Man and His God, probably composed during the Isin-Larsa period.[14] A similar and difficult Akkadian composition, the Dialogue between a Man and His God, dates to the late Old Babylonian period.[15] The theme of the pious sufferer culminated in three Akkadian literary compositions of the latter part of the second millennium. The Sufferer's Salvation was found at Ugarit but certainly originated in Babylon, since the sufferer pleads with the god Marduk.[16] The elaborate poem *Ludlul bēl nēmeqi* ("Let me praise the Lord of Wisdom")[17] and the Babylonian Theodicy,[18] cast in the form of a dialogue between the sufferer and a friend, both portray a pious man afflicted with feelings of dejection, abandonment, even paranoia. Because of the

---

13. There is a substantial secondary literature on the biblical motif of the pious sufferer and its Mesopotamian parallels. A bibliography is compiled by Gerald Mattingly, "The Pious Sufferer: Mesopotamia's Traditional Theodicy and Job's Counselors," in *The Bible in the Light of Cuneiform Literature: Scripture in Context* (ed. William W. Hallo et al.; Ancient Near Eastern Texts and Studies 8; Lewiston, N.Y.; Edwin Mellen Press, 1990), 3:305–48.

14. Partial translation with references to previous literature by Jacob Klein in *COS* 1.573–75.

15. *Editio princeps* by Jean Nougayrol, "Une version ancienne du 'juste souffrant,'" *RB* 59 (1952): 239–50. Translation with references to previous literature by Benjamin R. Foster in *COS* 1.485; and in *Before the Muses,* 1:75–77. Study by Wilfred G. Lambert, "A Further Attempt at the Babylonian 'Man and his God,'" in *Language, Literature, and History: Philological and Historical Studies Presented to Erica Reiner* (ed. Francesca Rochberg-Halton; AOS 67; New Haven, Conn.: American Oriental Society, 1987), 187–202.

16. *Editio princeps* by Jean Nougayrol in *Ugaritica* 5 (1968), 264–73, with copy on p. 435, no. 162. Translation with references to previous literature by Benjamin R. Foster in *COS* 1.486; and in *Before the Muses,* 1:326–27.

17. For general information, see Dietz O. Edzard, "Ludlul bēl nēmeqi," in *RlA* 7:107. Main edition is Lambert, *BWL,* 21–62. Several further sources have been published since, notably by Donald J. Wiseman in *Anatolian Studies* 30 (1980): 101–7, and by Andrew R. George and Farouk N. H. Al-Rawi in *Iraq* 60 (1998): 187–201. Translation with references to previous literature by Benjamin R. Foster in *COS* 1.486–92, and *Before the Muses,* 1:308–25.

18. Main edition is Lambert, *BWL,* 63–91. Translation with notes and references to previous literature by Benjamin R. Foster in *COS* 1.492–95, and *Before the Muses,* 1:806–14.

intensity of the feelings expressed and the sophistication of its language and imagery, *Ludlul* represents the crowning achievement of this tradition. Yet there is no perceptible evolution throughout the second millennium in the answer given to the sufferer. In all cases the sufferer acknowledges his potential guilt, although he cannot discover the nature of his transgression. The answer lies in blind faith. The sufferer must praise his god until he relents. If the gods have sent punishment for no apparent reason, it is because we do not understand their purpose. The Babylonian Theodicy takes the problem to a more abstract level. The sufferer muses on the human condition more than on his own predicament and does not directly address the issue of his own guilt. Yet, in the end, the Theodicy provides the same explanation: "The mind of the gods is as remote as innermost heaven; it is most difficult to understand, and people do not know it" (XXIV, 256–57).

While the answer given to the pious sufferer remained basically the same throughout the second millennium, *Ludlul* and the Theodicy innovate not only in providing far more elaborate expositions of the problem but also in making their social and intellectual settings very explicit. In *Ludlul* the name of the protagonist is revealed as Šubšimešrê-Šakkan, and the story is set in the milieu of the court (I, 55–69). The sufferer of the Theodicy is an orphan who originates in a privileged and literate milieu and complains that scoundrels and social inferiors have taken precedence over him. His friend praises his wisdom (*nēmequ*), intelligence, and knowledge. The acrostic of the composition gives away his name as Saggil-kīna-ubbib and his profession as exorcist.[19] The Catalogue of Texts and Authors from the library of the Assyrian king Assurbanipal mentions the Theodicy, but the name of the author is lost and the name of the king under whom he lived is only partly preserved.[20] *Ludlul* also certainly originated in the milieu of the exorcists. The text is replete with rare technical terms for diseases otherwise found mostly in medical texts. Furthermore, the young man named UrNintinugga, who appears in a dream to Šubši-mešrê-Šakkan announcing his upcoming deliverance, is an exorcist. He even carries a tablet that presumably contains the incantations, rituals, and prescriptions required to cure him. The very name of that young exorcist, Ur-Nintinugga "Servant of Ur-Nintinugga," heralds his medical knowledge. Nintinugga ("the lady who revives the dead") was a name of Gula, the goddess of medicine and healing. The importance of *Ludlul* for the practice of exorcism is further reflected in the fact that, in the curriculum of Neo-Babylonian schools, the composition was studied in the second stage of learning, the one that was entirely

---

19. Lambert, *BWL*, 63: *a-na-ku sa-ag-gi-il-ki-[i-na-am-u]b-bi-ib ma-áš-ma-šu ka-ri-bu ša i-li ú šar-ri* "I, Saggil-kīna-ubbib, the exorcist, a worshiper of god and king."

20. Wilfred G. Lambert, "A Catalogue of Texts and Authors," *JCS* 16 (1962): 66, fragment K. 10802, restores the entry as follows: 1. [......... *lu*]-*uq-bi-ka* 2. [*an-nu-ú šá pi-i* ¹*sag-gil-ki-nam-ub-bi-ib ina tar-ṣi* ᶦᵈIM-IBIL]A-SUM ᵏᵘMAŠ.MAŠ ˡᵘUM.ME.A TIN.TIRᵏⁱ "[......... let] me speak to you. [This is according to Saggil-kīnam-ubbib, a contemporary of Adad-apl]a-iddina, the exorcist, the expert scholar from Babylon." The identification of the composition as the Theodicy seem almost certain, given that the first line still preserves the end of its incipit (*luqbika*).

devoted to the *āšipūtu*, the craft of the exorcist, and prepared students to specialize in the higher intellectual disciplines.[21]

How must we explain this sudden involvement of the exorcist, the *āšipu* (or *maš-maššu*), in the field of wisdom at the end of the second millennium, and why does the art of medicine then find a place in a literary genre that seems a priori to have little in common with it? To answer this question, we must examine the Mesopotamian etiology of diseases. Disease and sickness were essentially caused by gods or malevolent spirits. Either a demon or a deity who had become hostile was the direct cause of the disease, having implanted it in the body of the patient, or the personal god had abandoned the worshiper, thereby causing discomfort, anguish, and eventually sickness. Such an etiology of diseases implies that therapeutics were not sufficient to cure the patient unless he was reconciled with his personal god or the malevolent powers who had caused sickness were exorcized.[22] Therefore, when compositions about pious sufferers insist that the various physical ailments afflicting the worshiper are the result of divine punishment, they only develop this general notion. Being afflicted with an actual disease, the sufferer cannot rely exclusively on his own resources, on his individual piety, and blind faith in the gods. He must seek a cure and resort to a medical expert, a professional and learned mediator. This is the great innovation of *Ludlul*. It is the first wisdom text that connects physical disease and divine abandonment in such a manner as to require medical knowledge of the highest order to cure the sufferer.

But where is that medical knowledge to be sought? The oldest branch of Mesopotamian medicine was the *asûtu*, "the craft of the physician," and the word *asû*, "physician," refers in the early corpus of Mesopotamian medical texts to a surgeon and herbalist who practiced a form of medicine that is variously characterized as traditional, empirical, or practical. During the second millennium, however, another form of medical knowledge appeared alongside, and partly in conjunction with, the *asûtu*. This was the *āšipūtu*, "the craft of the exorcist." I must immediately emphasize that the *āšipu*, the exorcist, practiced a craft that included several other fields besides medicine. He was really a polymath. By the late second millennium, the exorcist had become the most important medical practitioner, especially when magical procedures were involved. He was also responsible for carrying out rituals such as the *šu'illa*s, which are known exclusively from first-millennium libraries, yet probably originated in the Middle Babylonian period. The *šu'illa*s were essentially incantation prayers accompanied by rituals performed by an exorcist to reconcile a worshiper with his

---

21. Petra D. Gesche, *Schulunterricht in Babylonien im ersten Jahrtausend v. Chr.* (AOAT 275; Münster: Ugarit Verlag, 2000), 172–98, for a description of the second stage of learning (*zweite Schulstufe*); the inclusion of *Ludlul* is discussed on pp. 173 and 183, with a list of manuscripts on p. 814.

22. The Mesopotamian etiology of diseases, particularly in light of the Diagnostic Handbook (the Series SA.GIG), is well summarized in a recent article by Nils P. Heeßel, "Diagnosis, Divination and Disease: Towards an Understanding of the Rationale Behind the Babylonian *Diagnostic Handbook*," in *Magic and Rationality in Ancient Near Eastern and Graeco-Roman Medicine* (ed. H. F. J. Horstmanshoff and Marten Stol; Studies in Ancient Medicine 27; Leiden and Boston: Brill, 2004), 99.

estranged god. The feelings expressed in the prayers are very much the same as the ones we find in compositions about pious sufferers, that is to say, praise of the deity, sense of guilt, ignorance of the fault committed, feelings of dejection, paranoia, abandonment, bodily ailments and disease, and especially a desperate longing for the deity to relent—in sum, a range of sentiments also expressed in a number of biblical psalms, with the notable difference that *šu'illa*s, because of their nature as incantations, are often repetitive and formulaic. The two great wisdom texts from Mesopotamia, *Ludlul* and the Theodicy, both created in the milieu of the exorcists, only present more sophisticated philosophical expositions of the religious emotions expressed in *šu'illa*s. This makes the exorcist as much a doctor of the mind and soul as of the body.

The rise of the exorcist must also be understood within the context of the redefinition of scholarship and the reclassification of intellectual disciplines in Babylonia during the latter part of the second millennium. By the Kassite period the Old Babylonian institution of the *edubba* had all but disappeared, and with it much of the Sumerian literature that formed the curriculum of scribes. Schools in the late periods provided young scribes only with basic training. Specialized education and training in scholarship were available in the temple, the palace, or the private homes of learned families. Beyond the basic profession of scribe, higher scholarship was now divided into three main disciplines: the *āšipūtu*, "craft of the exorcist," the *kalûtu*, "craft of the lamentation singer," and the *bārûtu*, "craft of the diviner." Each discipline had its own curriculum and corpus of texts. The easiest discipline to define is the *bārûtu*. Babylonian divination was entirely based on the belief that omens were signs sent by the gods to express in cryptic terms their intentions to humans. The role of the diviner was to interpret these signs, often by provoking their appearance within a specific ritual context. Omens were not binding; they were only warnings. Once an evil omen had been identified and correctly interpreted, the most important task was to neutralize it, to avert its potentially damaging effects. It is at this point that the exorcist, the *āšipu*, stepped in with the performance of a *namburbû*, a ritual designed to cancel the effects of that omen.[23]

Performing *namburbû*s was only one of the many tasks of the exorcist. I just pointed out that he was also a magician and incantation priest who could reconcile the ailing worshiper to his deity with the performance of a *šu'illa* ritual. Thus, generally speaking, the role of the exorcist was to palliate the punishments sent by the gods, be they evil omens, diseases, or other symptoms of divine abandonment. The third discipline, the *kalûtu*, is clearly defined in a colophon from the library of Assurbanipal. In this colophon the king makes the following claim: "I wrote on tablets, according to copies from Assyria and Babylonia, the wisdom (*nēmequ*) of the god Ea, the series

23. Stefan M. Maul, "How the Babylonians Protected Themselves Against Calamities Announced by Omens," in *Mesopotamian Magic: Textual, Historical, and Interpretative Perspectives* (ed. T. Abusch and K. van der Toorn; Ancient Magic and Divination 1; Groningen: Styx, 1999), 123–29, provides a concise and insightful survey of these rituals, which are edited with extensive notes and commentaries in his monograph, *Zukunftbewältigung: Eine Untersuchung altorientalischen Denkens anhand der babylonisch-assyrischen Löserituale (Namburbi)* (Baghdader Forschungen 18; Mainz am Rhein: Verlag Philip von Zabern, 1994).

of the *kalûtu*, the secret knowledge of the sages, which is suited to quiet the heart of the great gods."[24] This statement clearly defines the purpose of the *kalûtu* and the role of the *kalû*, the lamentation singer, which was to appease the hearts of the angry gods with the singing of laments and the performance of rites of intercession. It must be noted that the Assurbanipal colophon classifies the *kalûtu* as a form of *nēmequ*, of wisdom, and that other sources apply the same label to the *āšipūtu* and the *bārûtu*. Indeed, other colophons from the library of Assurbanipal classify the *bārûtu* as the *nēmequ* of the gods Šamaš and Adad,[25] and the Catalogue of Texts and Authors ascribes the entire authorship of the *āšipūtu* and *kalûtu* to Ea, the god of wisdom.[26] This means that in late Mesopotamia, a vast portion of the corpus of learned texts fell within the general category of wisdom, although modern scholars would be reluctant to identify most of these texts as sapiential literature.

A further conclusion that emerges from this survey is that, by the end of the second millennium B.C.E. and the beginning of the first, intellectual life in Mesopotamia had become focused largely on the need to mediate between gods and humans. The humanistic scribal education of the *edubba* had given way to a theological education. Texts of almost every genre fulfilled one sole purpose: the acquisition by experts of a higher wisdom of practical nature that served to alleviate the suffering of worshipers in their absolute dependence on the gods. In Mesopotamia this theological shift of wisdom is further emphasized by the fact that exorcists, lamentation singers, and diviners played a significant role in the cult and belonged to the privileged caste allowed to enter the sanctuary and hold prebends in the temple. In this context the exorcistic medicine of the *āšipu* was really, if I may coin the term, a theological medicine. In light of this, it may be no coincidence that the best-known figure in the development of the *āšipūtu*, Esagil-kīn-apli, lived in the period when literary texts exposing the plight of the pious sufferer reached their most refined expression.

According to later tradition, Esagil-kīn-apli was the compiler and editor of *Sakikku*, the Diagnostic Handbook.[27] He was also remembered as systematizer of one of the two practices of the *āšipūtu* recognized by the Compendium of the Exorcist.[28]

---

24. Hermann Hunger, *Babylonische und assyrische Kolophone* (AOAT 2; Kevelaer: Butzon & Bercker; Neukirchen-Vluyn: Neukirchener, 1968), 102, colophon no. 328, lines 13–16 (Assurbanipal Type o).

25. Hunger, *Kolophone*, 100–101, colophon no. 325, line 3. The attribution of the *bārûtu* to Šamaš and Adad and its classification as a form of *nēmequ* is also clearly stated in the Enmeduranki tradition.

26. Lambert, "Catalogue," 64–65, lines 1–4.

27. Irving L. Finkel, "Adad-apla-iddina, Esagil-kīn-apli, and the Series SA.GIG," in *A Scientific Humanist: Studies in Memory of Abraham Sachs* (ed. Erle Leichty et al.; Occasional Publications of the Samuel Noah Kramer Fund 9; Philadelphia: University Museum, 1988), 143–59, discusses all the data on Esagil-kīn-apli. The Handbook is edited most recently by Nils P. Heeßel, *Babylonisch-assyrische Diagnostik* (AOAT 43; Münster, Ugarit Verlag, 2000).

28. The Compendium of the Exorcist, now known from several duplicates from Assyria and Babylonia dating to the first millennium, is edited most recently by Mark J. Geller, "Incipits and Rubrics," in *Wisdom, Gods and Literature: Studies in Assyriology in Honour of W. G. Lambert* (ed. A. R. George and I. L. Finkel; Winona Lake, Ind.: Eisenbrauns, 2000), 242–58. The second part of the Compendium (lines 27–

Esagil-kīn-apli allegedly lived during the reign of Adad-apla-iddina (1068–1047 B.C.E.) of the Second Dynasty of Isin and was the chief expert scholar (*ummânu*) of Sumer and Akkad, which means that he must have worked in close collaboration with the king. One potentially significant fact in this connection is that Adad-apla-iddina claimed a special relationship to the medicine goddess Nin-Isinna. He rebuilt her temple Egalmaḫ at Isin,[29] and in a set of brick inscriptions found at Ur calls himself son (dumu) of Nin-Isinna and son-in-law (mu$_{10}$-ús-sá/*ēmu*) of the moon god Nanna.[30] Comparable devotion to the goddess is unrecorded for other members of that dynasty, even though it was firmly associated with the city of Isin in ancient historiography. It is therefore conceivable that Adad-apla-iddina commissioned Esagil-kīn-apli to compile the Diagnostic Handbook mainly because he was a personal devotee of the goddess of healing.[31]

Ludlul ranks as the pious-sufferer text that is the most resolutely set within the context of exorcistic medicine. It is also the one most likely to have been composed in the cultural milieu that saw the compilation of the Diagnostic Handbook and the systematization of the *āšipūtu* by Esagil-kīn-apli and his school. However, it cannot be dated more precisely than to the last two centuries of the second millennium. The later tradition, on the other hand, apparently claims that the author of the Theodicy, the exorcist Saggil-kīna-ubbib, also lived in the reign of Adad-apla-iddina, but the matter is somewhat complicated. Our only sources for this dating are the Catalogue of Texts and Authors and the Uruk List of Rulers and Sages. As I pointed out earlier, the entry in the Catalogue is poorly preserved and has been restored on the basis of the acrostic of the Theodicy and the data from the Uruk List. The Uruk List gives the names of three *ummânu*s who lived in that period. The first one is clearly Esagil-kīn-apli, but problems arise with the two entries that follow:

16. [*ina tar-ṣi* …] ⌈LUGAL :⌉ ¹*é-sag-gil-ki-i-ni*-IBILA *um-man-nu*
   "[At the time of] king […] the *ummânu* was Esagil-kīn-apli."

17. [*ina tar-ṣi*] ᵈIM-⌈IBILA⌉-SUM LUGAL : ¹*é-sag-gil-ki-i-ni-ub-ba um-man-nu*
   "[At the time of] king Adad-apla-iddina, the *ummânu* was Esagil-kīn-ubba";

---

43) is devoted to Esagil-kīn-apli's version of the *āšipūtu*. The Compendium and the role of Esagil-kīn-apli are discussed at length by Jean Bottéro, *Mythes et rites de Babylone* (Paris: Librairie Honoré Champion, 1985; repr. Geneva: Slatkine Reprints, 1996), 65–112.

29. Frame, *Rulers of Babylonia*, 57–58, inscription B.2.8.7.

30. Frame, *Rulers of Babylonia*, 60–61, inscriptions B.2.8.10 and B.2.8.11.

31. Direct royal patronage of the series is further suggested by the last line of the colophon edited by Finkel, "Adad-apla-iddina," 148–50, lines 31'–33', which enjoins the *āšipu* to put his diagnosis at the disposal of the king: "[Let the *āšipu*] who makes the decisions, and who watches over people's lives, who comprehensively knows SA.GIG and Alamdimmû, inspect (the patient) and check (the appropriate series), [let him ponder], and let him put his diagnosis at the disposal of the king."

18. [*ina tar- și*] ^{Id}NÀ-NÍG.DU-ÙRI LUGAL : ¹*é-sag-gil-ki-i-ni-ub-ba*-LU *um-man-nu*

"[At the time of] king Nebuchadnezzar (I), the *ummânu* was Esagil-kīn-ubba-LU."

What are we to make of these names, are they one and the same? Saggil was the colloquial form of Esagil, the temple of the god Marduk in Babylon. Therefore, are Esagil-kīn-ubba and Esagil-kīn-ubba-LU necessarily spellings for Esagil-kīn-apli, or is it equally likely that they could be incorrect renderings of Saggil-kīna-ubbib? The text is evidently corrupt, and it cannot be taken too seriously in light of the other fanciful claims it puts forward.[32] However, the possibility of confusion between the names Esagil-kīn-apli and Saggil-kīna-ubbib was real, which leads one to suspect that these two contemporary exorcists with similar sounding names and who both allegedly lived under king Adad-apla-iddina, were considered to be one and the same person in some currents of the later tradition. Contrary to Esagil-kīn-apli, the name Saggil-kīna-ubbib belongs to an extremely rare type. In fact, the name Saggil-kīna-ubbib is unique, being attested only in the name of this author and lists of personal names copied in Neo-Babylonian schools, where it almost certainly occurs as a reference to the author.[33] It probably means "the Esagil temple has cleared the just." Such a name appears quite programmatic in the context of the tradition of the pious sufferer, especially *Ludlul*, where the sufferer is cleared by the god Marduk as he passes through the gates of the Esagil temple. One therefore suspects that it might have been an alternative name for Esagil-kīn-apli, a "born-again" name adopted in recognition of his deliverance and used as nom de plume.[34] One always bears in mind of course that ancient traditions of authorship are always suspect to some degree. Yet it seems clear that in the native view the Second Dynasty of Isin, in particular the reign of Adad-apla-iddina, was remembered as epochal in the elaboration of the *āšipūtu*. The movement that linked exorcism, medicine, spiritual healing, and philosophical reflection into one coherent

---

32. These two entries present a few incongruities. Nebuchadnezzar I reigned two generations before Adad-apla-iddina but is listed after him in the list. The irregularities in the spellings of the two names cannot be satisfactorily explained. One can attribute the mistakes to poor hearing if the list was dictated, or, if it was copied, to the existence of a previous manuscript that was damaged or corrupt. However, other names in the list are generally carefully written, and this raises the possibility that the name Saggil-kīna-ubbib was intentionally deformed to make it sound like Esagil-kīn-apli. The form Esagil-kīn-ubba-LU seems particularly puzzling. LU could be a substitution for LÚ, which is a possibility in that period. However, the word *ummânu* in the preceding and following entries is not prefixed with that determinative. Therefore, the scribe might be playfully proposing to equate the two figures by making the last part of the name *ubbalu* sound like IBILA, the logogram for *aplu*. Another possibility is that LU should be read IB!, the two signs being very similar in that period, and this would give a more convincing spelling of the name Esagil-kīna-ubbib (*ub-ba-ib*).

33. This was proposed by Lambert, *BWL*, 64. See Gesche, *Schulunterricht*, 89, for references to the name in school texts, where it is spelled *é-sag-ìl-ki-i-ni-ub-bi-ib* and *é-sag-ìl*-GIN-*ub-bi-ib*.

34. One must point out, however, that Esagil-kīn-apli was from Borsippa according to the tradition, and Saggil-kīna-ubbib from Babylon.

view very likely culminated in that period to produce masterpieces of scholarship and wisdom literature.

The setting of wisdom literature in the milieu of the *āšipūtu* is also fully in agreement with the cultural context of late Mesopotamian civilization. All the works listed in the Catalogue of Texts and Authors, when not ascribed to a god or mythical being, are attributed to a famous exorcist, lamentation singer, or diviner, the former two groups being by far the most prominent. For instance, the Epic of Gilgamesh is attributed to the exorcist Sîn-lēqi-unninni, and the Disputation between the Poplar and the E'ru Tree to the exorcist Ur-Nanna, an *ummânu* from Babylon.[35] Interest in authorship, tradition, and the pedigree of great scholars and their works is peculiar to the late periods, when prominent urban families began to wear patronyms. These patronyms consisted of the names of real or imaginary ancestors, some of them well-known sages. Obsession with lineage induced scholars to trace the origins of their knowledge further back in time, eventually to the mythical period before the flood. By appropriating antediluvian knowledge, expert scholars came into direct competition with kings, who until the late periods were alone in openly claiming a privileged link to primeval knowledge. This revisionist process initiated by the intellectual elites emerges into full light in a text from the library of Assurbanipal belonging to the Enmeduranki cycle. As discussed earlier, the scribes of King Nebuchadnezzar I celebrated their ruler as refounder of civilization after the flood by making him a descendant from Enmeduranki, who filled in this case the role traditionally assigned to Ziusudra. The text from the library of Assurbanipal also relates how the gods Šamaš and Adad appointed Enmeduranki as king in Sippar in antediluvian times and taught him the art of divination. It also adds, however, that Enmeduranki taught in turn the same arts to the men of Nippur, Sippar, and Babylon.[36] The text continues with stating that the diviner who qualifies to serve before Šamaš and Adad belongs to a distant lineage and is also an offspring of Enmeduranki, king of Sippar. The implication of this text is that now not only the king could lay a claim to antediluvian knowledge, but learned men as well.

The appropriation by scribes and scholars of an antediluvian wisdom formerly the privilege of kings led to the creation of a tradition of antediluvian sages. This tradition eventually merged with that of antediluvian kings in the form of parallel lists, such as the ones preserved in Berossus and the Uruk List of Rulers and Sages, where each antediluvian king is paired with an antediluvian sage. The purpose of such lists is obvious. The learned classes projected back into mythical times their role as royal advisors. Such a role is known mostly from Neo-Assyrian sources in the form of lists of kings and their expert advisors (*ummânu*)[37] and from the official correspondence of the Sar-

---

35. Lambert, "Catalogue," 66–67, VI: 10 (Sîn-lēqi-unninni); and VI: 14 (Ur-Nanna).

36. The text is published by Lambert, "Enmeduranki," 132–33.

37. The pairing of kings with *ummânus* is found in some king lists edited by Albert K. Grayson, "Königslisten und Chroniken," *RlA* 6:116–21 (King List 12 = Synchronistic King List) and 122–23 (King List 14 = Synchronistic King List fragment), which both give the names of *ummânus* of Assyrian kings. The

gonid court that documents the key role of scholars of all disciplines as royal counselors. Scholars now claimed as much of a connection to the ultimate source of wisdom, the gods and primeval sages (*apkallus*), as the king himself. The king did not
relinquish his position, however. In a colophon from his library, King Assurbanipal
claims to have been endowed with the wisdom (*nēmequ*) of Nabû, the god of the
scribal art, a reference to his alleged mastery of writing. Scholars still praised the king's
wisdom, sometimes comparing him to an *apkallu*. In the letter SAA 10, 174, Marduk-
šum-uṣur, the chief diviner of Assurbanipal, addresses him as follows: "The god Ashur,
in a dream, called the grandfather of the king, my lord, an *apkallu*. (Therefore) the
king, lord of kings, is the offspring of an *apkallu* and of Adapa. You have surpassed the
wisdom (*nēmequ*) of the Apsû and of all scholarship (*ummânūtu*)."[38] The choice of
words in this address is quite significant. The Apsû was the abode of the god Ea and
the locus from where all wisdom originated. The mythical sage Adapa was equated in
the first millennium with the antediluvian *apkallu* U'anna, known from the writings
of Berossus by the name Oannes. The Catalogue of Texts and Authors lists the works
of U'anna-Adapa in second position, just after those of the god Ea. This reflects a
hierarchy accepted by Berossus, who claims that Oannes was the first antediluvian
sage, and by the Uruk List of Rulers and Sages, which also puts him in the initial position. Marduk-šum-uṣur praises the king for his inherited wisdom, yet affirms obliquely
that wisdom ultimately resides with scholars.

What is the implication of this? Simply that antediluvian kings are no longer the
ultimate source of wisdom after Ea. Their place has been largely usurped by antediluvian sages. Antediluvian wisdom is only exceptionally given to kings, who normally must seek it from their advisor who have a privileged connection to the god Ea
and U'anna-Adapa. The king can now even be censored for unauthorized claims to
wisdom. This happened in the sixth century with Nabonidus, whose idiosyncratic
views on religion and ritual apparently provoked widespread anger among clerics. The
Verse Account of his reign parodies his self-praise in the assembly of scholars in a passage that is a reverse image of the praise of Assurbanipal and his grandfather Sennacherib in SAA 10, 174: "He would stand in the assembly and praise h[imself] (as
follows): 'I am wise (*enqēk*), I am learned, I have seen hi[dden things]. (Although) I
do not know how to write, I have seen secret [knowledge]. The god Sahar has
re[vealed] everything to me. I (even) surpass in all wisdom (*nēmequ*) the series Uskar-
Anu-Enlil, which Adapa compiled' (Verse Account, col. V, 8'–13')."[39] Nabonidus is
rebuked for not having listened to his scholars and advisors, the legitimate source of

---

usual formula is RN, PN *ummânšu*. These lists are also discussed by Simo Parpola, *Letters from Assyrian
Scholars to the Kings Esarhaddon and Assurbanipal. Part II: Commentary and Appendices* (AOAT 5/2; Kevelaer: Butzon & Bercker; Neukirchen-Vluyn: Neukirchener, 1983), 448–49.

38. Simo Parpola, *Letters from Assyrian and Babylonian Scholars* (SAA 10; Helsinki: Helsinki University Press, 1993), 136–37. Discussion of this motif with other examples are quoted in Beate Pongratz-
Leisten, *Herrschaftswissen in Mesopotamien* (SAAS 10; Helsinki: Helsinki University Press, 1999), 310.

39. New edition by Hans-Peter Schaudig, *Die Inschriften Nabonids von Babylon und Kyros' der Großen*
(AOAT 256; Münster: Ugarit-Verlag, 2001), 563–78.

knowledge, and for claiming his own god, the lunar deity Sahar, as the source of wisdom instead of Ea. Indeed, the superior status of expert scholars is clearly spelled out in another wisdom text from the first millennium, the Advice to a Prince, which warns the ruler against dismissing their advice: "Should he not pay heed to the scholars, the land will rebel against him (line 5)."[40]

The great wisdom texts of late Mesopotamian culture originated in the milieu of expert scholars who were practitioners of one of the great disciplines of cuneiform learning, chiefly the *āšipūtu*. Some of these scholars rose in the courtly hierarchy and became royal advisors. The correspondence of the Assyrian kings of the Sargonid dynasty amply documents the overwhelming presence and influence of exorcists, lamentation singers, diviners, astronomers, and other specialists at court. But how must we assess the place of sapiential literature within the larger Mesopotamian tradition of wisdom, the *nēmequ*? In the Ur III and Old Babylonian periods, when the *edubba* and its teachers dominated intellectual life, wisdom literature belonged to the common heritage of the scribes and served to perfect their rhetorical training. This was the primary function of proverbs, disputations, fables, and all other genres of scribal training literature. The scholars who controlled the great scribal academies such as those of Nippur were sometimes called upon to put their talents in the service of rulers, composing hymns in their praise as well as other texts that promoted their vision of a unified monarchy of Sumer and Akkad under the governance of wise and compassionate kings endowed with *nēmequ* by the god Ea. This is the context in which such compositions as the Instructions of Shuruppak and the Instructions of Ur-Ninurta were created. They view mythical and historical kings as the primary holders of wisdom after Ea and celebrate the king in his role as bringers of culture.

In the late periods of Mesopotamian civilization the social and intellectual context in which wisdom literature flourished changed substantially. Scribes, scholars, and royal advisors gained an influential place at court and invented traditions that put them on a par with the king in the intellectual and religious leadership of their culture, a role that became even more prominent with the demise of the last native Mesopotamian monarchy in 539 B.C.E. The practitioners of the great disciplines of the *āšipūtu*, *kalûtu*, and *barûtu* exerted a virtual monopoly on higher learning. The corpus of technical literature that formed the core of their practice became dominant in the cuneiform mainstream. They also authored much of the wisdom literature of the later periods. These compositions raise some of the same philosophical issues addressed by Hebrew and Egyptian wisdom literature, and for that matter by Greek philosophers. Yet their authors firmly believed that in the end the answer must lie only with the gods, who are the ultimate cause and remedy. This is where their role became crucial, because their disciplines focused on mediating between the gods and the world of humans. The craft of the exorcist was especially important. His role was to prevent the punishments sent by gods and demons and cure their effects, eventually reconcil-

---

40. New edition with the Nippur duplicate by Steven W. Cole, *The Early Neo-Babylonian Governor's Archives from Nippur* (OIP 114; Chicago: University of Chicago Press, 1996), 268–74.

ing the patient with his personal deity. All his activities, especially those related to medicine, must be understood with this theological framework in mind. Exorcistic medicine could cure only if the gods relented. Here compositions about pious sufferers clearly delineate the boundary between the respective efficacy of divine and human agency. In the Sufferer's Salvation from Ugarit and in *Ludlul*, visits to the exorcist are to no avail until Marduk decides to relent. Then, and only then, can the exorcist apply his cure effectively, only then does he become a skilled craftsman.[41] The Mesopotamian tradition insists that the *āšipūtu* originated with the god Ea, Marduk's father. Its transmission since the beginning of time through a long line of *apkallu*s and *ummânu*s ensured that the exorcist and scholar could partake in Ea's original wisdom, that of a skilled craftsman, a craftsman of the soul.

It is obvious from this survey that, in the Mesopotamian view, wisdom occupied a considerably wider sphere than the one we intuitively ascribe to it. The Mesopotamian concept of *nēmequ* was a far-reaching one, with implications in all areas of life and for all domains of intellectual activity. Wisdom originated with gods and bringers of culture, who imparted it to humans. It included not only all skills required to lead a proper life but also ritual prescriptions and a number of arcane disciplines and esoteric arts accessible to a restricted elite of specialists who acted as mediators between the divine and human worlds. Within such a context, the place of sapiential literature seems limited, all the more so when we consider that the Sumerian and Akkadian words for wisdom occur rarely in wisdom literature, and never as general labels to categorize such texts. Babylonian wisdom literature, especially in its later developments, appears to some degree to be an epiphenomenon. That literature is mostly devoted to the expression of existential problems that were common to many ancient civilizations. It portrays a dissonance, the alienation of individuals who come to the realization that the world is ruled by mysterious powers implicitly demanding absolute devotion and blind faith, but where retribution is arbitrary. That the need to write such texts should have emerged in a society that provided virtually no space for the expression of individuality is a remarkable fact in and of itself. This is due in part to the prominence gained by the learned classes, who often depicted themselves as the protagonists of compositions of pious sufferers. Intellectuals occupy the entire space of the discourse in these texts, in that they appear as both sufferer and media-

---

41. This is reflected in formulas that the exorcist uttered while performing his duty, such as "The incantation is not mine, it is the incantation of Ea and Asalluhi, the incantation of the exorcist of the gods, Marduk" (various references listed in *CAD* Š/III, s.v. *šiptu*, p. 88). The exorcist even acted as an impersonator of the god Marduk, as the series *bīt mēseri* tells us: "the incantation is the incantation of Marduk, the exorcist is the very image of Marduk" (quoted in CAD A/II, s.v. *āšipu*, p. 431b, lex. section). That Marduk was the real exorcist is well conveyed in a literary text published by Wilfred G. Lambert, "Marduk's Address to the Demons," *AfO* 17 (1954–1956): 310–21, with additions in *AfO* 19 (1960): 114–19; Marduk, as Asalluhi, addresses demons in the first person and proceeds to expel them. See also the recent discussion by Wilfred G. Lambert, "Marduk's Address to the Demons," in *Mesopotamian Magic: Textual, Historical, and Interpretative Perspectives* (ed. Tzvi Abusch and Karel van der Toorn; Ancient Magic and Divination 1; Groningen: Styx, 1999), 291–96, in which the question of impersonation by cultic specialists is briefly discussed.

tor, as patient and doctor. Yet the themes addressed in these compositions, for all their universal appeal, must not be separated from the broader theological system that the Babylonians elaborated in the late second and early first millennia. Only within this context can we grasp their uniqueness. They represent the highest literary formulation of certain aspects of a complex and deeply original theology that mustered all forms of science and knowledge to build a channel that could reach onto the transcendental world of the gods.

Why Wisdom Became a Secret: On Wisdom as a Written Genre

Karel van der Toorn

Introduction

In this contribution on Mesopotamian wisdom I shall argue that the cuneiform tradition witnesses a significant shift in the concept of wisdom between the second and the first millennium B.C.E. Wisdom—*nēmequ* is the word the Babylonians use—is originally a human virtue that expresses itself in the form of legal verdicts, intelligent counsel, and pithy sayings. In the course of time, however, "wisdom" became a virtue solely of the gods. Experience as the soil of wisdom gave way to revelation as its ultimate source. This development takes place at the turn from the second to the first millennium B.C.E. A major witness to the transformation is the Standard Babylonian version of Gilgamesh.

Gilgamesh as Wisdom

The Epic of Gilgamesh is a piece of cuneiform literature that we do not immediately associate with wisdom. An epic is an epic, not wisdom. Yet the Epic of Gilgamesh is truly wisdom literature, not only by modern standards,[1] but also from the perspective of the Neo-Assyrian scribes and scholars.

We owe our knowledge of the scribal classification of Gilgamesh to the so-called Catalogue of Texts and Authors.[2] The Catalogue is not a library catalogue, but a canon of works fit for instruction and memorization. The scholars responsible for this work were concerned with ordering the classics of the scribal curriculum. Their classification of the literature is by presumed antiquity, which is also an order of authority.

---

1. Andrew F. George, *The Babylonian Gilgamesh Epic: Introduction, Critical Edition and Cuneiform Texts* (Oxford: Oxford University Press, 2003), 1:32–33.

2. Wilfred G. Lambert, "A Catalogue of Texts and Authors," *JCS* 16 (1962): 59–77.

Gilgamesh is among the last works on the list, alongside Etana,[3] the Series of the Fox,[4] Sidu,[5] and the Series of the Poplar.[6] These are all wisdom texts and, as such, works of human inspiration attributed to human authors—as opposed to the corpus of exorcism, divinely inspired, and attributed to Ea.

The Old Babylonian Edition of Gilgamesh

The Epic of Gilgamesh has a long history. It is best known from its two major editions, the Old Babylonian from about 1600 B.C.E, and the Standard Babylonian, presumably written some five hundred years later, around 1100 B.C.E. The differences between the two editions are important. They reflect a change in the concept of wisdom.

The Old Babylonian edition of Gilgamesh was called, after its opening line, "Surpassing all other kings."[7] It is a third-person account of the great deeds of Gilgamesh. The epic conveys the message that the way to a good life requires acceptance of one's mortality and the mental disposition to moderately enjoy the good things in life. This is the wisdom Gilgamesh eventually attains on his search for immortality after the death of Enkidu. The counsel of the tavern-keeper Siduri, spoken to Gilgamesh as he is near the end of his journey, sums up the wisdom message of the epic:

> O Gilgamesh, where are you wandering?
> You cannot find the life that you seek:
> When the gods created mankind,
> For mankind they established death,
> Life they kept for themselves.
> You, Gilgamesh, let your belly be full,
> Keep enjoying yourself, day and night!
> Every day make merry,
> Dance and play day and night!
> Let your clothes be clean!
> Let your head be washed, may you be bathed in water!

---

3. The attribution of Etana to the class of wisdom texts is based in part on the presence of the Fable of the Serpent and the Eagle now integrated into the epic; see J. V. Kinnier Wilson, *The Legend of Etana: A New Edition* (Warminster: Aris & Phillips, 1985); Wolfgang Röllig, "Literatur," *RlA* 7/1–2:48–66, esp. 60 sub §4.7.6 a).

4. See Burkhart Kienast, *Iškar šēlebi: Die Serie vom Fuchs* (Freiburger Altorientalische Studien 22; Stuttgart: Steiner, 2003).

5. See Irving L. Finkel, "On the Series of Sidu," *ZA* 76 (1986): 250–53: "All titles [of the series] preserved are in Sumerian, and all that are identified belong in the sphere of proverbs or related wisdom-type literature" (253).

6. See *BWL*, 164–67.

7. After the opening line of the epic known from the Old Babylonian Pennsylvania tablet. See Stephen Langdon, *The Epic of Gilgamesh* (Publications of the Babylonian Section, University Museum, University of Pennsylvania 10/3; Philadelphia: University of Pennsylvania Press, 1917), rev. iii 35.

Gaze on the little one who holds your hand,
Let a wife enjoy your repeated embrace!
Such is the destiny [of mortal men,] (...)
OB Sippar tablet, iii 1–14[8]

The Standard Babylonian Edition of Gilgamesh

In the Standard Babylonian edition of the epic, the scribal editor, identified by tradition as Sin-leqe-unninni, has added a prologue of twenty-eight lines. Line 1 in the Old Babylonian version has become line 29. The new prologue emphasizes that the epic is about wisdom (*nēmequ*).[9] It pictures Gilgamesh as a man who obtained secret wisdom, inaccessible to others:

> *ša nagba īmuru [i]šdi māti*
> *[ša kulla]ti īdû kalama hass[u] (. . .)*
> *[nap]har nēmeqi ša kalāmi [īhuz]*
> *[ni]ṣirta īmurma katimta iptē*
> *ubla ṭēma ša lām abūbi*

He who saw the Deep, the country's foundations,
Who knew everything, was wise in all matters! (...)
He learnt the sum of wisdom of everything.
He saw what was secret, discovered what was hidden,
He brought back a message from before the flood.
Gilg. I i 1–2.6–8[10]

The theme of the prologue returns at the end of the text, in tablet XI. There the author reveals what kind of wisdom Gilgamesh did learn. It is not the wisdom of the tavern-keeper, whose *carpe-diem* counsel has disappeared from the text. In the Standard Babylonian version, Gilgamesh receives his wisdom from Utnapishtim, also known as Atrahasis, the hero who survived the flood.

The episode of the encounter with Utnapishtim was already part of the epic in Old Babylonian times, as the last part of the so-called Sippar tablet suggests. Yet it is evident from the literal correspondence between the closing lines of tablet XI and lines 18–23 of the prologue (XI 322–28 = I i 18–23) that the editor who added the prologue was also responsible for a thorough revision of tablet XI (that is, the corre-

---

8. Translation by George, *Babylonian Gilgamesh Epic*, 1:279.

9. By presenting the epic as a *narû*-inscription (I i 24–28), the Standard Babylonian editor puts the text "in the key of wisdom," as William L. Moran observes, "The Epic of Gilgamesh: A Document of Ancient Humanism," *Bulletin of the Canadian Society for Mesopotamian Studies* 22 (1991): 15–22, quotation on 19; repr. in *The Most Magic Word* (ed. R. S. Hendel; CBQMS 35; Washington, D.C.: Catholic Biblical Association, 2002).

10. See George, *The Babylonian Gilgamesh Epic*, 1:538–39.

sponding passage in the Old Babylonian edition). He added the account of the flood, the homily by Utnapishtim, and an epilogue.[11]

In the Standard Babylonian version of Gilgamesh's encounter with Utnapishtim, the latter refers to secrets in a manner reminiscent of the prologue:

> luptēka ᵈGilgameš amat niṣirti
> u pirišti ša ilī kâša luqbika

> Let me disclose, O Gilgamesh, a matter most hidden,
>   To you I will tell a secret of the gods.
>   (Gilg. XI 9–10, repeated in 281–82)

The first secret Utnapishtim discloses is the tale of the flood. This is the story that is referred to in the prologue as "a message from before the flood." The second secret is the existence of a plant of rejuvenation. We know that the single specimen of this plant gets lost to Gilgamesh. Swallowed by the snake, it will only reinvigorate the ophidians; humans cannot escape their destiny.

The language of secrecy that the Standard Babylonian edition uses is largely rhetorical. There is no real secret involved. The story of the flood is not a secret in the sense that it was preserved only among a small elite of initiates. The Old Babylonian Atrahasis story was well known. Nor is the existence of a rejuvenating plant a secret; it is a familiar theme of folklore, presumably known to the ordinary Babylonian, just as most Israelites were familiar with the tale about a "tree of life."

HIDDEN WISDOM REVEALED

Even if the language of secrecy is largely rhetorical, the Standard Babylonian edition of Gilgamesh reflects a significant shift in the concept of wisdom. Whereas in the Old Babylonian edition wisdom is human knowledge painstakingly acquired by a lifetime of experience, a half millennium later wisdom becomes divine. Where once a female inn-keeper had been the voice of wisdom, now a deified hero from before the flood has taken her place. The wisdom he discloses is out of the reach of ordinary mortals. It is far off, both in space and time. According to Gilgamesh, this secret wisdom is from before the flood, that is, chronologically remote, and beyond the ocean and the waters of death, in the realm of Utnapishtim. In other words, it is chronologically and topographically distant. Unless revealed, this wisdom remains hidden.

SECRET KNOWLEDGE AS SUPERIOR WISDOM

The new concept of wisdom encapsulated in the Standard Babylonian edition of the epic presents wisdom as knowledge from before the flood. It is transmitted to Gil-

---

11. According to George, *Babylonian Gilgamesh Epic*, 1:32–33, the Sin-leqe-unninni version added a prologue and an epilogue, as well as the flood narrative and the homily by Utnapishtim.

gamesh by the antediluvian hero Utnapishtim. He reveals it as one reveals a secret. The shift, from wisdom by experience to wisdom by revelation, turns wisdom into a new category of knowledge. It is henceforth associated with such traditional scholarly lore as exorcism, astrology, and divination. These disciplines—and more specifically the manuals in which they written down—are qualified in colophons and elsewhere as "wisdom of Adapa," "wisdom of the Sages," or "wisdom of Ea." Ea is the god Ea, ruler of the subterranean waters, source of wisdom and skill. The "Sages" are the apkallus, the mythological counselors from before the flood. Adapa is their figurehead. Celebrated for his wisdom in the myth of Adapa,[12] he is known as the founding father of civilization under the name Oannes-Uanna.[13]

If the Standard Babylonian version of the Gilgamesh epic is indeed from the late second century B.C.E., it is one of the first witnesses to a new paradigm of wisdom. That the heroes from before the flood were exceedingly wise was common knowledge already in Old Babylonian times; witness the Atrahasis poem and the myth of Adapa. Yet it was only in the first millennium that scribes established a connection between the antediluvian heroes and the main scholarly disciplines. All the written scholarly lore came to be defined as the "wisdom of Adapa."

The fact that the first millennium B.C.E. adopted a new paradigm of wisdom is also evident from the royal inscriptions. That the king is by definition "wise" is a commonplace that goes back to the third millennium. Royal wisdom once referred to intelligence and legal acumen. The Laws of Hammurabi are proof of that king's wisdom. By the first millennium, however, wisdom as a royal attribute came to be understood in the sense of knowledge of the secret lore entrusted to Adapa. Neo-Assyrian kings were the first ones to compare themselves with Adapa. The traditional phrase has it that they were "as wise as" or "wiser than" Adapa. Assurbanipal loses no opportunity to claim that the wisdom of Adapa pales in comparison to his scholarship. Sennacherib and Esarhaddon before him made similar statements. Witness the Verse Account of Nabonidus; the topos was taken over by the Neo-Babylonian kings.[14]

According to the wisdom of the Old Babylonian Gilgamesh, there is no remedy against death but the enjoyment of the present. Such ephemeral joy is no solace to the poet of the Standard Babylonian version. He proposes a superior wisdom by holding out secret knowledge from before the flood as the only antidote to death. Such knowledge does not prevent anyone from dying, but its comfort is more satisfying than hedonism.

The preoccupation with knowledge, secrets, and wisdom from the divine realm reflected in the Standard Babylonian version of Gilgamesh and in first millennium

12. See Shlomo Izre'el, *Adapa and the South Wind: Language Has the Power of Life and Death* (Mesopotamian Civilizations 10; Winona Lake, Ind.: Eisenbrauns, 2001).

13. Jonas C. Greenfield, "apkallu," *DDD*, 72–74.

14. For a convenient survey of passages on the king as paragon of wisdom, see Ronald F. G. Sweet, "The Sage in Akkadian Literature: A Philological Study," in *The Sage in Israel and the Ancient Near East* (ed. John J. Gammie and Leo G. Perdue; Winona Lake, Ind: Eisenbrauns, 1990), 45–65, esp. 51–57.

colophons of scholarly texts tells us something about the mindset of Mesopotamian scribes and scholars of the time. They saw themselves as the heirs of Adapa and the other apkallus from before the flood. Presenting their scholarship as a secret vouchsafed to them exclusively, they boasted of their status of initiates. Though they had never made such extraterrestrial journeys as Gilgamesh and Adapa, they had, nonetheless, access to the wisdom disclosed to these giants.

The Scribalization of Wisdom

It is one thing to observe the shift in the Mesopotamian concept of wisdom; it is something else to explain it. Why did wisdom become a "secret"? The most likely explanation, it seems to me, is related to writing. As the traditional lore became literature, it came to be considered a secret. Tales had once been told from one generation to the next; scholarly lore had once circulated only by word of mouth. In the first millennium, however, the transmission of tradition took the form of formal instruction in the context of the formation of scribes. The apprentice scribes had to familiarize themselves with the texts of the classics, both of the narrative tradition (myths, epics, and the like) and of scholarly knowledge (exorcism, astrology, divination, and the like). They were taught to value these texts as scribal secrets not to be divulged beyond the circle of initiates.

We owe our knowledge about the scribal attitude toward written texts to the secrecy colophons appended to first-millennium copies.[15] The common form of the colophon contains four elements: it qualifies the text as "secret" (*pirištu* or *niṣirtu*); confines its transmission to the milieu of the "experts," or "initiates" (*mūdû*); prohibits its divulgation to the "nonexpert" (*la mūdû*); and says that the tablet is the "sacred property" or "taboo" (*ikkibu*) of the gods. One late example (Hellenistic era) illustrates all four elements:

> Mathematical table, divine wisdom, secret of the [great go]ds, secret of the scholars. One expert may show it to [another expert]; the non-expert is not allowed to [see it. Sacred property] of Anu, Enlil, and [Ea, the great gods.][16]

Such colophons are appended to all kinds of texts. They qualify the entire body of scribal tradition as a matter of experts only, to be kept away from the public eye. The art of writing itself is a secret. When Assurbanipal claims that he has learned "the hid-

---

15. For a survey, see Rykle Borger, *Handbuch der Keilschriftliteratur* (Berlin: de Gruyter, 1975) 3:119 §108; Paul-Alain Beaulieu, "New Light on Secret Knowledge in Late Babylonian Culture," *ZA* 82 (1992): 98–111, esp. 110–11.

16. Hermann Hunger, *Babylonische und assyrische Kolophone* (AOAT 2; Kevelaer: Butzon & Bercker; Neukirchen-Vluyn: Neukirchener Verlag, 1968), 42 no. 98. For a study of the form of the colophon, see Borger, "Geheimwissen," *RlA*, 3:188–91, esp. 189.

den secret of the complete scribal art,"[17] he is echoing the esteem in which the scribes themselves held their professional lore.

It may seem strange to us that writing should turn a text into a secret; to us writing is a means of communication.[18] This difference in the appreciation of the effects of writing is related to the rate of literacy of the society in which we live. If over 95 percent of the population is literate, owing to the inability of the common folk to read, writing is indeed a means of dissemination. Yet in a society that is by and large illiterate, the written word is an object of veneration. To them, writing is more a means of encrypting a message than a means of communication and preservation.

It is difficult to assess just how secret the "wisdom" of the scribes actually was. How much of a mystery were the mystery cults of the Hellenistic era to the people of the time? Modern authors on the subject do not believe that there was any real mystery involved. As Walter Burkert suggests, the language of secrecy served to provide the participants in the cult with a feeling of being privileged and gave them the identity of initiates.[19] The secret itself was only a rhetorical reality. Much the same holds true of the professional secrets of various medieval guilds. It is hard to believe that matters were very different in ancient Mesopotamia. Most people were familiar with the adventures of Gilgamesh; the story of the flood was no secret at all. Only specialized knowledge, like that of the astrologer or the diviner, was confined to scholarly circles, but one doubts whether the rest of the population greatly cared. The secret nature of their knowledge was a matter of importance primarily to the scribes themselves. It gave them a sense of superiority with little effect outside their own circles.

WISDOM AND WRITING IN GILGAMESH

I have argued that the new concept of wisdom is closely related to writing. If wisdom came to designate a secret lore, it is because the written tradition was the exclusive province of the professionals of writing. The new wisdom is scribal wisdom.

It deserves to be noted that the Standard Babylonian version of Gilgamesh reflects both the emergence of the new vision of wisdom and its link to writing. Many commentators have observed that the editor reshaped the concept of wisdom; few of them have made the connection, however, with the role the prologue assigns to writing. The prologue, which the editor of the Standard Babylonian version has added, turns Gilgamesh into a man who "learnt the sum of wisdom of everything, who saw what was secret, discovered what was hidden." The same prologue also turns Gilgamesh

---

17. *niṣirtu katimtu kullat ṭupšarrūtu*; see Maximilian Streck, *Assurbanipal und die letzten assyrischen Könige bis zum Untergang Ninevehs* (Vorderasiatische Bibliothek 7; Leipzig: J. C. Hinrichs, 1916), 2:254:13; cf. Rykle Borger, *Beiträge zum Inschriftenwerk Assurbanipals* (Wiesbaden: Harrassowitz, 1996), 187.

18. Cf. Plato 2 *Ep.* 314c: "[I]t is not possible that what is written down should not get divulged. The greatest safeguard is to avoid writing and to learn by heart" (LCL).

19. See, e.g., Walter Burkert, "Der geheime Reiz des Verborgenen; Antike Mysterienkulte," in *Secrecy and Concealment: Studies in the History of Mediterranean and Near Eastern Religions* (ed. Hans G. Kippenberg and Guy G. Stroumsa; SHR 65; Leiden: Brill, 1995), 79–100, esp. 96–97.

into a kind of scribe. Not only is he the hero of the poem, he is also the one who put it down in writing.

Like other famous kings such as Sargon and Naram-Sin, Gilgamesh is presented in the prologue as the author of an autobiography. The name for the genre is *narû*, literally, a "stele with inscription." According to line 10 of the prologue, Gilgamesh "set down on a stele all his labors." The word used is, indeed, *narû*. Toward the end of the prologue the audience is invited to

> [Take] the tablet-box of cedar,
> [release] its clasp of bronze!
> [Lift] the lid of its secret,
> [pick] up the tablet of lapis lazuli and read out
> the travails of Gilgamesh, all that he went through.
>
> Gilg. I i 24–28

The transformation the editor effects in the prologue is thus twofold. He changes the concept of wisdom that informed the Old Babylonian version of Gilgamesh. At the same time, he transforms a tale about Gilgamesh into a document written by Gilgamesh. As a result, the wisdom that the new version promotes is wisdom in writing. It is accessible only to those who can pick up the tablet and read.

CONCLUSION

It could be demonstrated that the development of the Mesopotamian concept of wisdom has a striking parallel in biblical literature. The interpretation of the written Torah as wisdom personified, known from such texts as Sirach 24 and Baruch 3, allowed Jewish scribes to make a comparable shift in their concept of wisdom. Wisdom from experience—your own and that of others—was the traditional concept of wisdom; wisdom by revelation takes its place in the Persian and the Hellenistic era. The principal difference with Mesopotamia is the emphasis that this new wisdom is, precisely, no secret. Having come down from above, it is accessible to all.[20]

The parallel with the Bible deserves to be explored at far greater length. For the time being, I must confine myself to a recapitulation of the main points of the argument about Mesopotamian wisdom. The Epic of Gilgamesh is not only a masterpiece of Mesopotamian narrative art; it also allows us, owing to the preserved text of two successive editions, to trace a major development in the concept of wisdom. The comparison between the Old Babylonian and the Standard Babylonian versions of

---

20. See my "Sources in Heaven: Revelation as a Scholarly Construct in Second Temple Judaism," in *Kein Land für sich allein: Studien zum Kulturkontakt in Kanaan, Israel/Palästina und Ebirnari für Manfred Weippert zum 65. Geburtstag* (ed. Ulrich Hübner and Ernst Axel Knauf; OBO 186; Fribourg: Universitätsverlag; Göttingen: Vandenhoeck & Ruprecht, 2002), 265–77.

Gilgamesh reveals a fundamental change. Where wisdom used to be a spoken counsel by someone with experience, it turned into knowledge of secrets from distant days. Such knowledge could be obtained only through disclosure by some god or an exceptional human being. Since it had been committed to writing—by Gilgamesh and others—it was accessible to the scribal elite. Wisdom became scribal wisdom—knowledge of mysteries that had little to do with the practical realities of everyday life.

PART TWO

Studies in Babylonian Wisdom Texts

An Allusion to the Šamaš Hymn in Dialogue of Pessimism

Victor Avigdor Hurowitz

The comic composition *arad mitanguranni*,[1] often called Dialogue of Pessimism, is known to contain several literary allusions as might be expected in a work of social satire.[2] So, for instance, line 76 most likely refers to a line appearing at the beginning and end of the Ninevite recension of the Gilgamesh Epic, while lines 83–84 are, according to Lambert, "a certain quotation of a proverb" (*BWL*, 140).[3] This brief note will identify and discuss another allusion that, although appearing immediately before the passage containing the already cited allusions, has not been noticed previously.[4]

---

1. The initial signs are not preserved, nor are there any known colophons. This title, restored on the basis of the formula repeated at the head of each round in the dialogue, although most likely, is still only a conjecture.

2. All agree that the composition is philosophical, but whether and to what degree it is meant to be solemn, pessimistic, humorous, cynical, or satirical is still a matter of scholarly deliberation. For two recent discussions see J. Bottéro, "The Dialogue of Pessimism and Transcendence," in *Mesopotamia: Writing, Reasoning, and the Gods* (trans. Z. Bahrani and M. Van De Mieroop; Chicago: University of Chicago Press, 1992), 251–67; E. Greenstein, "Wise Guys Even at Night: The Babylonian Dialogue between a Master and His Servant and the Book of Ecclesiastes," *Beit Mikra* 44 (5759 [1999]): 97–106 (Hebrew).

3. See R. C. Van Leeuwen, "The Background to Proverbs 30:4aα," in *Wisdom, You Are My Sister: Studies in Honor of Roland E. Murphy, O. Carm., on the Occasion of His Eightieth Birthday* (ed. Michael L. Barré; CBQMS 29; Washington: Catholic Biblical Association 1997), 102–20, esp. 103.

4. For links with other Mesopotamian and ancient Near Eastern wisdom literature, see E. Ebeling, MVAG XXIII/2 (1919), 50–70; and cf. E. A. Speiser, "The Case of the Obliging Servant" *JCS* 8 (1954): 98–105 = *Oriental and Biblical Studies: Collected Writings of E. A. Speiser* (ed. J. J. Finkelstein and M. Greenberg; Philadelphia: University of Pennsylvania Press, 1967), 344–68. Lines 70–78, to be discussed below, and especially the doing of *usâtu* and its rewards have been compared to Counsels of Wisdom ll. 61–65 (*BWL*, 102) by Nili Samet in her soon-to-be-published Hebrew University MA thesis on the Dialogue of Pessimism. Samet also discusses the relationship between Dialogue of Pessimism, ll. 70–78, and the related passage in the Sun God Hymn, but in a way somewhat different from our treatment. I am grateful to Ms Samet for showing me the relevant portions of her work. As part of a paper read on June 20, 2005 at the Hebrew University's Institute for Advanced Studies, Dr. Nathan Wasserman discussed several previously undetected resonances of the Gilgamesh Epic in the Dialogue.

In the eighth, hyperpenultimate, round in the dialogue between the master and his obliging slave (lines 62–69), the master suggests that he gives (a loan) as a creditor, *ummâna luddin*. True to form, and as he does throughout the conversation, the slave confirms and justifies the master's wise program by saying *idin bēlī idin; ša ummâna inamdinu uṭṭassu uṭṭassuma ḫubulšu atri*; "Give, my lord, give! Someone who gives (a loan) as a creditor, his grain is his grain, while his interest is enormous," which means that one who makes a loan not only receives his capital back undiminished but adds to it. Equally true to form, when the master changes his mind, the servant finds equally strong reasons for the new but contradictory suggestion. People who borrow are inevitably ingrates, eating what they receive but cursing the hand that feeds them, and in the end destroying the master's profits. In the ninth, and next-to-last round of the dialogue, the master proposes *usâtam ana mātīša lūpuš*, "I shall perform a public benefit for my land," to which the servant responds, *epuš bēlî epuš; amēlu ša usâtam ana mātīšu ippuš šaknā usâtūšu ina qappat[5] ša Marduk*, "Do, my lord, do! A person who performs a public benefit for his land, his benefits rest in the basket of Marduk." According to B. Foster, "The idea may be that if one distributes largesse, the recipient is the god himself, so good will thereby accrue to the giver."[6] When the master again reverses himself, the servant is right there to agree, this time saying that everyone dies in the end and no one remembers whether the person had been a benefactor or a malefactor.

I would like to propose that these two rounds of the dialogue allude to, derive from, and react to two consecutive and similarly phrased passages in the great Hymn to Šamaš (*BWL*, 121–38), namely lines 118–21 and 122–27. These passages describe the actions as well as the rewards of two types of people. First, in lines 118–19 we find *ummâni kīnu nādin šēm ina kabrim pān ušattâr dumqu ṭāb eli Šamaš balāṭa uttar*, "The honest merchant/creditor who weighs out (loans of) corn by the maximum standard, thus multiplying kindness; it is pleasing to Šamaš, and he will add to his life." This is followed by a promise that he will enlarge his family, gain wealth, and proliferate effusively (120–21). The ensuing passage (122–23) starts, *ana ēpiš usât dumqi la mūdû ṣilipti muštenû šaplāti ina misdari šaki[n ina maḫrīka?]*, which Foster, following a suggestion of M.-J. Seux has translated, "For the man who does virtuous deeds, who knows not fraud, the man who always says what he means, there will be [...]."[7]

The similarities between the texts are striking and pervasive. Both the Dialogue and the Hymn speak first about giving (a loan) as a creditor, using collocations of *ummânu* and *nadānu*. Significantly, of the hundreds of attestations of *ummiānu/ummânu*, which is the general term for artisan and the like, these two passages are the only ones listed by W. von Soden as meaning "Geldverleiher, money

---

5. For the reading *qappat* rather than *kippat*, see W. von Soden, *TUAT* III/1, 162 n. 73.

6. B. Foster, *Before the Muses: An Anthology of Akkadian Literature* (3d ed.; Bethesda, Md.: CDL Press, 2005), 923–26, esp. 925 n. 1.

7. B. Foster, *Before the Muses*, 632; M.-J. Seux, *Hymnes et prières aux dieux de Babylonie et d'Assyrie* (Paris: Cerf, 1976), 59 nn. 64–65.

lender" (*AHw* 1415b s.v. *ummiānu* 7).[8] This is followed immediately in both texts by *epēš usâti,* "doing a good deed" or "public service." In both cases, a reward is antici-pated for what is done. This reward is expressed with the verb *atāru,* "gain," "increase," in the case of the loan, and *šakānu,* "to be present/placed," in the instance of the pub-lic benefit. In both texts, one of the parallel passages mentions that a god, Šamaš or Marduk, will be pleased by what the person does, which implies that there will also be some reward.

Although the passages in the Dialogue are shorter and more condensed than the parallel ones in the Hymn, the structural parallels, similarity in content, and identi-cal rare phraseology indicate dependence between the two texts.[9] And it is clear that the satirical composition is dependent on and alludes to the liturgical work. Although one cannot speak strictly of citations, one may certainly say that language and ideas of one composition are borrowed and incorporated into the other and used in a novel way. The shared elements are not mere clichés, as some of the other commonalities have been characterized, but points of contact between two specific literary works.

The intertextual allusion at issue is interesting in itself and contributes to the lit-erary sophistication of Dialogue of Pessimism, but it also has significance for the nature of the respective compositions.

On the one hand, it shows that the Šamaš Hymn, or one of its components,[10] was actually read, perhaps studied in school, and considered important enough to respond to satirically. The Hymn's importance and popularity were evidenced previously by the numerous manuscripts indicating that it was frequently copied and studied. Citing it in another literary work, however, and a satirical one in particular, emphasizes that its message was considered one to be taken seriously. The servant cites it positively, prof-fering it as good advice, as it was certainly intended to be, and supporting with it the master's initial whim, but then he just as easily turns it on its head, criticizes it, and shows its inherent weakness or futility, as he has done with everything else. Moreover, citation of the Hymn to the Sun God may also indicate that it or some part of it was regarded or used in antiquity not as a liturgical work but as a didactic or reflective composition, and lends certain justification to its inclusion in a present-day collection of wisdom literature.

---

8. The meaning of the word is determined by um.mi.a in *MSL* 1, 36/7, [56–57]; 82, [59] in which the Akkadian is restored as *ummiānu* and translated *Kapitalist.* The context is words relating to loans.

9. Speiser, "Obliging Servant," n. 23, already states, "Note also such links with Akkadian proverbs as the sequence *epru* and *usâtu* in K. 33851 obv. ii 13, 16 (*Proceedings of the Society of Biblical Archaeology* [1916] 133)". He refers to the Babylonian recension, but the allusion discussed here involves the main, Assyrian recension.

10. This is not the place to discuss the dates of either of the compositions. Foster places the Šamaš Hymn in what he calls the Mature Period (1500–1000 B.C.E.), while he dates Dialogue of Pessimism to his Late Period (1000–100 B.C.E). According to Lambert, "Either the [Šamaš] hymn is the result of a late reworking of an early text, or it is an original late composition based on early materials," or it has an early kernel that has been much expanded. He considers the Kassite period as probably too early for the extant version (*BWL,* 123).

On the other hand, identification of this allusion shows that Dialogue of Pessimism not only lampoons recognizable human types, behavioral patterns, and social situations but also takes jibes at specific literary compositions. It functions, therefore, not only in a social context but in a literary one as well and is addressed to people who can be expected to be familiar with the Hymn to the Sun God.

The Wisdom of Šūpê-amēlī—
A Deathbed Debate between
a Father and Son

Victor Avigdor Hurowitz

Mesopotamian writings of a didactic or reflective nature frequently designated as "wisdom literature" are well known to Assyriologists and biblicists, largely thanks to corpora such as Wilfred Lambert's *Babylonian Wisdom Literature* (hereafter *BWL*), Willem Römer and Wolfram von Soden's fascicle in *TUAT*, Edmond Gordon's and Bendt Alster's collections of Sumerian proverbs, and articles or monographs on various individual works.[1]

This article will discuss a relatively lengthy Akkadian wisdom composition that is only now gaining wide recognition.[2] A single, partial manuscript was published by

---

1. Wilfred G. Lambert, *BWL*; Willem H. Ph. Römer and Wolfram von Soden, *Weisheitstexte* I (*TUAT* III/1; Gütersloh: Gerd Mohn, 1990); Edmond Gordon, *Sumerian Proverbs: Glimpses of Everyday Life in Ancient Mesopotamia* (New York: Greenwood Press, 1968); Bendt Alster, *Proverbs of Ancient Sumer: The World's Earliest Proverb Collections* (Bethesda, Md.: CDL Press, 1997); idem, *Wisdom of Ancient Sumer* (Bethesda, Md.: CDL Press, 2005); Claus Wilcke, "Philologische Bemerkungen zum Rat des Šuruppag und Versuch einer neuen Übersetzung," *ZA* 68 (1978): 196–232; Åke W. Sjöberg, "The Old Babylonian Eduba" in *Sumerological Studies in Honor of Thorkild Jacobsen on his Seventieth Birthday June 7, 1974* (Assyriological Studies 20; ed. Stephen J. Lieberman; Chicago: University of Chicago Press, 1976), 159–80.

2. This is not the place to discuss the well-known question of whether the term "wisdom literature" is a term suited to literature outside the Bible in general and Mesopotamian writings in particular. See *inter alia BWL*, 1; Giorgio Buccellati, "Wisdom and Not: The Case of Mesopotamia," *JAOS* 101 (1981): 35–47. Suffice it to say that the composition studied here combines elements resembling in form and content "didactic wisdom literature" as exemplified in the biblical Book of Proverbs, and "reflective wisdom literature" as found especially in Ecclesiastes. Moreover, the counsels are presented in a family situation as are the admonitions in Proverbs. In addition, the values promoted by this composition are universal, for although they may reflect values of a certain social rank they are not bound by any particular ethnic background or religious beliefs. Although the protagonist's wisdom is attributed to divine gift, there is no indication that the advice itself or the response to it derive from divine revelation and are not a product of individual or shared, group experience. Missing from this composition is identification of "wisdom" with religious piety, fear of God, and the like, a feature unique to biblical wisdom literature and unknown in the supposed parallel genres in Egypt and Mesopotamia.

Jean Nougayrol in 1968,[3] but new editions and studies based on additional manuscripts began appearing only in the last decade. The text's structure, rhetorical devices, and some biblical parallels were studied by Duane E. Smith and John Khanjian in *Ras Shamra Parallels* II, and its language was discussed in studies of western peripheral Akkadian.[4] The work appeared eight years too late for inclusion in *BWL*, but it appears in Benjamin Foster's *Before the Muses* and is mentioned briefly in Michael Fox's commentary on Proverbs.[5] For some reason it was not included in *TUAT* from 1990 or in *Context of Scripture* from 1997, and even Lambert's 1995 article on new Mesopotamian wisdom literature does not mention it.[6] Even so, the text is finally becoming known, thanks to extensive studies of its literary structure, language, content, and message by Manfred Dietrich, Thomas Kämmerer, and Stefano Seminara.[7] Some of its ideas have already been compared with those of Ecclesiastes, and more will be said on this matter later.[8] In this paper I will present the text, analyze its literary form, content, unique message, and place in Mesopotamian wisdom literature, and offer some thoughts about similarities with biblical wisdom literature. I must stress that my study is only a preliminary one, and leaves much to be done before fully understanding all aspects of the work, including its relationship with biblical wisdom literature.

At the end of this article is a provisional English translation, one meant to provide no more than a preliminary, fluent reading and a general idea of the text's content.[9] The translation is divided thematically, and alternate renderings are indicated.

---

3. *Ugaritica V* (ed. Jean Nougayrol et al.; Mission de Ras Shamra 16; Paris: Imprimerie Nationale, Librarie Orientaliste Paul Geuthner, 1968), 273–90.

4. *Ras Shamra Parallels: The Texts from Ugarit and the Hebrew Bible* (ed. Loren R. Fisher; AnOr 50; Rome: Pontifical Biblical Institute, 1975), 2:216–47, 372–400; Wolfram von Soden. "Bemerkungen zu einigen literarischen Texten in akkadischer Sprache aus Ugarit," *Ugaritica V*, 189–95.

5. Benjamin Foster, *Before the Muses: An Anthology of Akkadian Literature* (3d ed.; Bethesda, Md.: CDL Press, 2005), 416–21 (the first two editions of this anthology contained only partial translations); Michael Fox, *Proverbs 1–9* (AB 18A; New York: Doubleday, 2000), 23, 428.

6. Wilfred G. Lambert, "Some New Babylonian Wisdom Literature," in *Wisdom in Ancient Israel: Essays in Honor of J. A. Emerton* (ed. John Day et al.; Cambridge: Cambridge University Press, 1995), 30–42.

7. Manfred Dietrich, "Der Dialog zwischen Šūpê-amēli und seinem 'Vater,'" *UF* 23 (1991): 33–68; Götz Kaydana, "Anhang: Die Hethitische Version," *UF* 23 (1991): 69–74; Manfred Dietrich, "Babylonian Literary Texts from Western Libraries," in *Verse in Ancient Near Eastern Prose* (ed. Johannes C. de Moor and Wilfred G. E. Watson; AOAT 42; Kevelaer: Butzon & Bercker; Neukirchen-Vluyn: Neukirchener, 1993), 41–67, esp. 52–62; Thomas R. Kämmerer, *šimâ milka: Induktion und Reception der mittelbabylonischen Dichtung von Ugarit, Emár und Tell el-ꜤAmârna* (AOAT 251; Münster: Ugarit-Verlag, 1998); Stefano Seminara, "Le Istrozioni di Šūpê-amēli: Vecchio e nuovo a confronto nella 'sapienza' siriana del Tardo Bonzo," *UF* 32 (2000): 487–529. I am grateful to my colleague Dr. Tova Forti for her assistance in reading Seminara's article and her enlightening comments concerning the text and study.

8. Augustinus Gianto, "Human Destiny in Emar and Qohelet," in *Qohelet in the Context of Wisdom* (ed. Antoon Schoors; BETL 136; Leuven: Leuven University, 1998), 473–79; Joseph Azize, "Considering the Book of *Qohelet* Afresh," *Ancient Near Eastern Studies* 37 (2000): 183–214, esp. 204.

9. See now Benjamin Foster, *Before the Muses*, 416–21. He notes that the text is often corrupt and difficult to understand and that his version contains much guesswork.

Words have been added as necessary for the purpose of fluency, and similarities to other texts, including the Bible, are noted. The translation, combining several manuscripts, is eclectic, and philological issues have not been addressed.

The name of the composition has not been preserved in the existing colophon, but scholars have called it the "The Instruction of Šūpê-amēli," or "A Dialogue between Šūpê-amēli and His Father" according to its content, form, and name of the main character, or *Šimâ milka* according to its first words. A composition called [*še-me-*]*e mi-il-kam* listed in an Old-Babylonian literary catalogue has been identified with this text.[10] But Seminara has questioned this identification, and, in fact, the appearance of this work in the Old Babylonian period is not consistent with the distribution of known manuscripts.

The composition is in Akkadian and exists in copies from sites outside Mesopotamia, including Ugarit, Emar, and Hattusa. The Hattusa manuscript contains a Hittite translation. The distribution of the manuscript, along with the rendition in another language, attests to the work's popularity in the mid-second millennium B.C.E., not in the Mesopotamian heartland but in the western periphery of the cuneiform *Kulturkreis*. The geographical and temporal proximity to Israel at the supposed time of its emergence raises special interest, and Smith already asserts that "the structure of biblical wisdom literature was already fully developed and available in Babylonian garb in the area of the Mediterranean basin even before the appearance of Israel."[11]

The work is structured as a dialogue between a father, who speaks first, and his son, who responds. Something similar is found in the Egyptian Instructions of Any.[12] Unfortunately, grammatical difficulties and damage to the manuscripts prevent determining with certainty whether Šūpê-amēli, whose name appears explicitly at the beginning of the text, is the father or the son. For the same reasons, it is impossible to know whether the first lines are said by the father to the son, or by the narrator addressing the reader or readers.[13]

---

10. A suggestion of Miguel Civil, "The Texts from Meskene-Emar," *AuOr* 7 (1989): 7, who refers to a line in Mark E. Cohen, "Literary Texts from the Andrews University Archaeological Museum," *RA* 70 (1976): 130–33.

11. *Ras Shamra Parallels*, 2:216–47, 372–400.

12. See Miriam Lichtheim, *Ancient Egyptian Literature: A Book of Readings. II: The New Kingdom* (Berkeley: University of California, 1976), 135–46.

13. In two manuscripts the sign preceding the name is broken or effaced, and it could have been either DIŠ, the determinative preceding masculine names, or the relative pronoun *ša*, "which." If it is the determinative, then Šūpê-amēli would be the son to whom the words are addressed. If it is the relative pronoun, then the father is the first speaker. The uncertainty about the reading raises a difficulty in parsing the first word of the text in particular and the introductory passage in general. If Šūpê-amēli is the father, then *šimâ* must be taken as the second-person singular imperative, and the composition is addressed to the readers and the first passage is said by the author. If Šūpê-amēli is the son, however, then *šimâ* means "listen to me (singular imperative + first-person indirect object pronominal suffix), your father," and the introductory passage is the father's exordium to his son. There is, in fact, reason to think that Šūpê-amēli is the son to whom the instructions are addressed, and that the problematic sign should be read as a determinative and *šimâ* should be translated "listen to me." To be precise, in line 3 there is no sign introducing the name, and if we read *ša* in the first line we would expect it to recur in line 3, because the expression *emqa milka*

In order to determine the composition's literary form beyond its formal nature as a dialogue, and in order to understand what its ancient author thought it to be, we must look at explicit internal evidence. The text ends with a colophonic title describing the text which went before:

> *Annû dabāba abu māru ištēniš dekû*
> This (the above dialogue) is the talk which the father and the son aroused.

This line undoubtedly refers to the conversation and adds nothing to what can be learned from a superficial reading of the text. *Dabāba dekû* means "argument," "dispute," or "competition," but no support from other Akkadian texts can be brought for any of these possibilities. The expression may function like Sumerian a-da-min₃ du₁₁/dug₄-ga, "dialogue," "argument," or "contest," which designates the well-known Sumerian debates, but the terms are not synonymous.[14] It might be pointed out, however, that *dabāba deku* is synonymous in primary meaning with Hebrew עורר מדנים in Prov 10:12: שנאה תעורר מדנים, "hatred stirs up strife."[15]

At the beginning of the son's reply, he refers to his father's instructions as *amātu*, "words," not a very revealing term. But the father's words are described in the beginning of the work with several more specific terms, including *milka*, "advice," *emqa milka*, "wise advice," *paraṣ/s ūmē aḫriāti*, "the law/decision of days to come," *dalāla*, "praise," and even *kapdata taslīta*, which means "a well-planned prayer." Dietrich explained *taslīta* as a form of *teslītu*, "prayer," and this interpretation is strengthened by the parallelism with *dalāla*, "hymn"; and even if "prayer" is not an appropriate term to depict advice to live by, the same applies to *dalālu*, "praise." Perhaps the description of advice as "praise" can be compared with Hammurabi's description of his Laws, which are *ana emqim ana tanādātim šūṣâ*, "but to the wise, they are praiseworthy" (xlix), namely, these counsels, like Hammurabi's laws, will bring praise to the son or anyone else who follows them (see Deut 26:19).

The son's reply ending the composition mentions the funeral arrangements for his father, indicating that the dialogue occurs near his father's death. If so, the father's words are a sort of ethical will. Perhaps we should compare the expression *paraṣ/s ūmē aḫriāti*, "law/decision of the last days," to Jacob's last words to his sons: "gather round so I can tell you that which will become you באחרית הימים" (Gen 49:1). Furthermore, several of the Egyptian instructions, such as those of Kagemni, Ptahhotep, Amenemhet to his son Sesostris, and Any, are also ethical wills.[16]

---

cannot be in construct state. Even so, the combination *šimâ milka*, which means literally "listen to me the advice, O Šūpê-amēli," is difficult, and in the second part of the introduction, the speaker is described in the third person, which strengthens the claim that the first lines are said by the author and that Šūpê-amēli is the father.

14. Line 6 reads *an bukri itta i milikšu*, "to the son his advice went out," and perhaps the verb *ittaṣi* from *waṣû* alludes to the term *tēṣētu*, which is the Akkadian term synonymous with the Sumerian a-da-min₃, "debate." See *AHw* 1475f. for the comparison a-da-min₃-di/-du₁₁-ga: (*waṣûm*).

15. Cf. Hebrew co-locutions of דין and דבר with Akkadian *dânu* and *dabābu*.

16. See Miriam Lichtheim, *The Old and Middle Kingdoms*, vol. 1 of *Ancient Egyptian Literature: A*

The father's words are a series of instructions to his son, each phrased in second person singular, and some followed by second- or third-person motive clauses. The preamble and instructions are in elevated style with poetic embellishments. The number of instructions is not clear; some have been lost, and it is difficult to know in every instance where one ends and the next begins. Dietrich identified about twenty-two instructions, while Seminara divides the same material into only sixteen.

The most important matter is, of course, the content and intent of the instructions and of the son's reply. The text is difficult to translate, and as one can see from the translation below, a literal translation is inelegant and at times incomprehensible. Moreover, the end of the father's words has not been fully preserved, so one cannot fully grasp the overall message of his counsel or know whether he summarized and synthesized it beyond the combined meanings of the individual instructions. At the same time, and in hope that our reading accords with the author's intent, it seems that we can understand the gist and overall tenor of a large portion of the instructions, even if we cannot claim full and precise comprehension.

As stated already, there are no less than sixteen instructions, and we can define the following topics:[17]

1. *Work the land rather than go on a journey; or the social advantages of going on a journey.
2. ** Don't frequent a tavern together with your friends.
3. **Don't belittle your friend or do him wrong.
4. ???Don't get involved in a court case, slander, and other matters.
5. Damages inflicted by a son.
6. ?Wicked behavior.
7. Don't endanger yourself because of pride.
8. ???Fear nothing.
9. **Guard your savings and your thoughts, especially from a nosey wife.
10. Don't respond to your detractors.
11. Don't dig a well at the entrance to your field, because others will benefit from it and you will incur a loss.
12. Mistaken purchases and misconceptions of which to be wary.
13. Don't buy a spruced up or ostentatious slave.
14. Don't be considerate of a morose tenant.
15. Protect the family wealth and your secrets from litigators.
16. Don't exchange the family house for a tent (summary and inclusion returning to the opening theme?).

According to this list, several instructions deal with proper behavior, especially toward friends (1, 2, 3, 6, 7, 10). Others relate to preservation of private and family

---

Book of Readings (Berkeley and Los Angeles: University of California Press, 1973), 59–61 [Kagemni], 61–80 [Ptahhotep], 135–39 [Amenemhet I].

17. Asterisks or question marks indicate the degree of certainty or uncertainty of the interpretations.

property, and apparently also of family secrets (9, 15, 16). The overall drift of the instructions is pragmatic. The father wants his son to fit into society, live a "normal" life, succeed materially, and preserve his inheritance and the integrity of the family property. Apart from a brief warning at the end of the sixth instruction not to offend a god who is not his own, the father's words hardly mention religious matters, and do not relate to the gods. Enlil-banda (Ea) is the source of wisdom; the human being is born with the help of Šamaš and Fire, and he is consigned to Ereškigal after his death; but the gods have no particular effect on his day-to-day circumstances or how he runs his life. Similarly, most of the instructions are practical and pragmatic, and it is difficult to discern any specific moral concern. One who disobeys the father's counsel endangers himself because of the natural outcome of his misdeeds, or disturbs the natural or social order, but does not infringe some absolute code of values of good and bad, just and unjust, etc. Even in the third instruction, doing wicked deeds is discouraged because an evildoer will suffer public punishment, and if there is some value judgment involved here it is not the primary consideration.[18] At the same time, the son is commanded not to get into trouble with others, to mind his mouth, avoid evil or ostentatious actions, and control his temper—all things that contribute to developing a desirable character.

The father's instructions have parallels in the Sumerian Instructions of Shuruppak and the Akkadian Counsels of Wisdom.[19] Not only is the repeated invocation "my son" common to these compositions; but they all take interest in matters of daily life, economy, good behavior, etc., and there are even some individual instructions similar in content and language. I would go so far as to say that were the father's instructions in *Šimâ milka* written together with the Instructions of Shuruppak or the Counsels of Wisdom it would be nearly impossible to separate them. Clearly, the instructions in the present composition spring from the same tradition that gave rise to the other works.

Nonetheless, ours is no routine composition, and the impression changes abruptly when examining the son's reply. This reply falls into five parts relating to the following:

1. human nature
2. birth
3. work and its profits
4. death and funeral and the father's inheritance
5. after death

---

18. Something similar can be found in the Book of Proverbs. So, for instance, in the admonition against banding together with wicked people in order to commit a robbery, the danger entailed is in the behavior of the conspirators one with another after completion of the crime (Prov 1:8–19). Even the warning against involvement with "foreign women" emphasizes the resultant heartbreak (Prov 5:11) and the wrath of a jealous husband (Prov 6:26–35) rather than ethical or religious compunctions.

19. Lambert, *BWL*, 96–107.

The son relates in his reply, albeit very briefly, to his father's advice. He touches immediately on the question of the essence of human life, pointing to man's nearly bestial wanderlust, which deprives him of rest. Man resembles a restless animal or beast who wanders about constantly (*murtappidu*). The father, at the beginning and end of his advice, recommends that the son stay at home or go into the field together with his friends, but the son claims that human nature, over which he in any case has no power, drives him so he cannot stay at home. It becomes clear that the father, as in accepted didactic wisdom, assumes man to have power over his own actions, for without such control there is no point in giving advice. The son rejects not only the advice but this assumption. In other words, not everything is in man's control.

Afterwards, while surveying the phases of life from womb to netherworld, the son comments on the worthlessness of property. Strangers take one's wealth, and fertility in the fields depends on rain that may or may not arrive. Also, a man cannot take his property with him to the grave, even if he has a luxurious funeral. Finally, a man's true, permanent house is not the grand dwelling he built himself during his lifetime but the hovel awaiting him after his death. Moreover, his "true" parents are not his birth father and mother but Ištar and Šamaš, who bore him, and Ereškigal, queen of the underworld, who will care for him when passing beyond the nothingness of this world and its material life. It turns out, then, that death renders worthless all human accomplishment, great as it may be. In effect, the son rejects his father's advice by saying that in the end there is no importance to the things that will befall a man, even if he heeds the pragmatic counsels promising success. The son is duly impressed by his father's wealth, acknowledging that the advice can attain its goals, but he questions the ultimate worth of these attainments.

If I have read this composition correctly and interpreted it as its author intended, it will be, to the best of my knowledge, a unique work of Mesopotamian literature. Sumerian and Akkadian collections of proverbs and didactic instructions parallel in essence and intent the words of the father in the present composition. We also encounter specific parallels with the Instructions of Shuruppak and the Counsels of Wisdom. On the formal side, the Babylonian Theodicy, the Dialogue of Pessimism, and the Debate poems are all couched as dialogues.

But, with all this, no other work criticizes the accepted didactic wisdom and its values. The closest thing to this composition is, perhaps, the Dialogue of Pessimism, in which the servant succeeds in justifying with equal merit opposing ways of behavior, thereby criticizing, albeit indirectly, the very possibility of distinguishing between good and bad and between the desirable and the undesirable.[20] In the Egyptian Instructions of Any, the son answers the father's instruction and a conversation ensues,

---

20. Lambert, *BWL*, 139–49. This composition has been studied recently by Edward Greenstein, "Wise Men Even at Night: The Babylonian Conversation between a Master and His Servant and the Book of Ecclesiastes," *Beth Miqra* 44 (5759): 97–106 [Hebrew] (= "Sages with a Sense of Humor" in this volume).

but the son does not question the truth and value of his father's statements but only questions his own ability to follow the advice because it is difficult.

But comparison of our composition with biblical wisdom literature, namely Proverbs, Job, and Ecclesiastes, shows some interesting lines of similarity, both formal and material.

1. The father's words are phrased in complex units resembling the multiversed sermonettes typical of Prov 22:17–24:22 and Proverbs 25–29, seriatim. Similarly, several instructions made of single verses are comparable with the bicolon adages found in Prov 10:1–22:16.

2. Several specific instructions have thematic parallels in Proverbs and Ecclesiastes.

3. The father addresses the son as *mārī*, "my son," as in Proverbs 1–9, Ahiqar, and in Mesopotamian compositions such as the Instructions of Shuruppak.

4. Šūpê-amēli's special wisdom is attributed to Enlil-banda, alias Ea, god of wisdom.[21] This resembles Prov 2:9: "For the Lord gives wisdom, from his mouth are knowledge and cunning." At the same time, however, the father's advice, as most of the instructions in Proverbs, does not derive from any special divine inspiration or revelation, but, rather, from individual and collective human experience of daily life.

5. As already stated, the father's advice is pragmatic, mundane, and not necessarily religious. This resembles what William McKane takes as the early, secular strand in Proverbs.[22] This conception is found in the additions to the Words of the Wise (Prov 24:23–34), "The Proverbs of Solomon Transmitted by the Men of Hezekiah" (Proverbs 25–29), and "The Words of Agur son of Yakeh" (Prov 30:7–33). In all these God is hardly mentioned, and it may resemble the primitive wisdom found in the book.

6. A dialogue in which the participants present opposing views of life is found in the Book of Job, although the questions debated by Job and his friends are questions of divine justice.

7. Everything mentioned so far is general. But although Ecclesiastes is not written as a dialogue, a type of dialogue does appear. This dialogue is Qohelet's internal struggle, which pits the wisdom tradition to which he was heir and in which he was educated against his own evaluation of reality derived from personal observation. This brings us to the most important similarity between this Akkadian composition and one particular book of the Bible. The Instructions of Šūpê-amēli is actually a conversation between a father who criticizes his son's behavior, trying to teach him the values current in society, as found in the Book of Proverbs, and a son who challenges the validity of the values as found in the Book of Ecclesiastes. The father encourages mate-

---

21. For this name, see Hans D. Galter, "Der Gott Ea/Enki in der akkadischen Überlieferung: Eine Bestandsaufnahme des vorhandenen Materials" (Ph.D. diss., Karl-Franzens Universität Graz 58, 1981), 26.

22. William McKane, *Prophets and Wise Men* (SBT 44; London: SCM, 1965), esp. 48–54.

rial and social success in life, as in one of the levels in the Book of Proverbs, and this is the old wisdom, the pre-Yahwistic stratum, according to McKane. This life resembles the life of wealth and happiness that Qohelet lived, examined, and criticized and which he ultimately found without absolute value. The son, even while admitting man's ability to succeed and get rich, contests the very value of this success, the value of possessions. In Qohelet's words, אין יתרון בכל עמלו, "There is no advantage in all his acquisitions." Moreover, the factor that nullifies the value of material success is death, which crouches at everyone's doorstep. In Qohelet's case as well, the value of property and success is erased and wiped out in the face of death. If so, this Akkadian work constitutes a precedent to the Book of Ecclesiastes and its critique of life on the one hand and accepted wisdom of life on the other.[23]

There is another matter. The son's response contains parallels to Psalm 49, a "wisdom psalm"(?), which compares man to a beast and emphasizes the nothingness of human accomplishments and wealth in particular when facing death. *Šimâ milka* presents the thoughts of Psalm 49 in refutation of Proverbs' orientation to success, and this combination creates exactly the contrast that gave birth to the Book of Ecclesiastes!

In summary, we have examined a pre-Israelite composition containing various elements known from Mesopotamian, biblical, and even Egyptian wisdom literature. The form of the father's instructions, the rhetorical devices employed, and their style resemble the instructions on wisdom in the Book of Proverbs. The values that the father preaches resemble those of the early strata of the Book of Proverbs. The use of dialogue as a vehicle to criticize accepted wisdom resembles that of Job. But above all else, the son's attitude to his father's counsel is like Qohelet's attitude to his wisdom heritage, which he examines and finds invalid.

In conclusion, the Book of Ecclesiastes criticizes accepted and widely held didactic wisdom. This intellectual approach, though developed at the twilight of the biblical period under the influence of proto-Hellenistic or Greek wisdom, fits well into a local tradition going as far back as the late second millennium B.C.E. Were Qohelet to read *Šimâ milka* he would certainly chuckle and remark (Eccl 1:10): יש דבר שיאמר ראה זה חדש הוא / כבר היה לעולמים אשר היה לפנינו.

THE INSTRUCTIONS OF/FOR ŠŪPÊ-AMĒLĪ
(*preliminary translation*)

Preamble
Hear the counsel (*milka*) [of] Šūpê-amēlī (or: Hear the counsel, O Šūpê-amēlī)

Whose ear Enlil-banda has opened (= to whom Ea has given wisdom)! //
(Hear) the wise counsel (*emqa milka*) (of) Šūpê-amēlī (or: Hear the wise counsel, O Šūpê-amēlī)

---

23. Both the son's words in this composition and the words of Qohelet end with the mention of death. According to Qohelet, the spirit will return to God who gave it (Eccl 12:7) and, according to the son, the dead are children of Ereškigal, goddess of the underworld.

To whom Enlil-banda has given an ear (= to whom Ea has given wisdom)!
From his mouth emerges the law (or: decision) of future days (*paraṣ/s ūmē aḫriāti*)
(cf. Gen 49:1);

> To mankind he says words of praise (*dalāla*) //
> To the son (first born?) his counsel (*milku*) emerges,
> He speaks words of well-planned prayer (*kapdata taslīta*) (or: he spoke the well-planned sarcasm).

The Father's Counsel

1. Work the land instead of going on a journey
*(or: the social advantages of going on a journey (cf. Šuruppak 170–71)**

My son,
At your side your month changes (or: By your hand your warehouse becomes a desert waste).
One who goes on a journey leaves his irrigated field (of his home)
At your side (or: by your hand) you […], you go. You will acquire an irrigated field of the desert;
O, my replacement (= my heir)!
Who is it whose wanderings are found with the wind in the open field? (= who walks alone in the field with only the wind?)
And you, together with a comrade, complete your quest—
One who goes with a friend, (his) head [is raised?] //
    One who goes with an army, weapons go with him. (cf. Eccl 4:9–12)

2. Don't visit a tavern with your comrades **

Don't enter, **O son**, a tavern/house of feasting! (cf. Eccl 7:2–4)
(It will[. . .] you, fattens the heart (= dims the minds; cf. Isa 6:10; Adapa 58–59))
Don't go, **O son**, with an army of talkers
(lest) you steal (place your hand on) rations //
    (lest) you smite your beer. (cf. Prov 23:29–35; 31:4–7)

3. Don't slander your friend or plan evil**

In a market, a passage way for throngs, do not bring your mouth (or: In a market of passage don't speak "thick things").
Don't slander a person to a friend // His lack of friendship will not leave his mouth.
You will receive punishment;
Early punishment (or: curses and invectives), (planting) a trap, treason, abuse of power without respite—to all (these) things do not set your sights!

4. Avoid judicial problems (broken)???

5. Damages caused by a son

To raise the head [...]
An immodest son is a distress [of his father] (cf. Prov 10:11; 15:20)//
     a tardy/retarded son will lose the family (property).
Every day his enhanced portion...[...] (or: each of his days is a loss for him, for he
     has already taken his profits).

6. Wicked behavior?

Mercy (or: a mother) not his [...] you shall not [...]
My son,
With plunderers do not eat ground flour! (or: with plunderers do not pillage
ground flour! (cf. Prov 1:5–11; 29:21)).
Impoverishing (or: subduing) the young with help of (or: simultaneously with) the
elderly don't do!
Do not speak derisively about a god to whom you have not made libation (= don't
act without respect to a god who is not your own).

7. Don't hurt yourself showing off

Even if every king will be your strength (or: let your strength be in every counsel)
(cf. Prov 20:18; 24:6)
With strongman do not fight!

Do not jump over a wide canal—
(lest you fall into the water and) chill yourself //
     (and) you will have a wound on your face
and you will feed your doctor a sacrificial lamb (= you will pay a lamb to the
doctor).

8. Fear nothing (broken)???

9. Guard your savings and your thoughts, especially from your wife **

To the woman you love open not your heart (thoughts) (cf. Mic 7:5).
Sea[l it] (your heart), even if she (your wife) is stubborn, even if she is suspicious
     (cf. Judg 14:16–17).
The gift in your sealed chamber [watch?]
(That which is (in your purse) your wife should not know/learn.)

Ever since our predecessors (ancestors) determined what came before us,
Our ancestors divided the regular sacrifices with the gods.
They drove in the bolt (of the treasure house), fixed the lock, sealed it in clay.
(And now) lock the sealed house! Drive in the bolt! Guard your house!
Be it your seal, be it the opening of your skull (your thoughts),
All that you see, leave in your heart //
　　　only if it is something you need, then give it to her.

10. Do not react to the provocation of your detractors (cf. Prov 11:12)

All the time, people are only anger for the gods (or: frustration for the gods).
Slander (lit., bitterness) from the mouth, leave! Don't hold (it in your heart)!
(But, if) issuing slander of the mouth you hold (in your heart), do not fear (= let your heart not throb),
(for) your innards will worry // the heart, your malicious words you will [...]

11. Don't dig a well at the entrance to your field
for others will enjoy it and you will bring loss upon yourself
(cf. Šuruppak 15–18)

At the head (entrance) of your field do not dig a well;
(But, if in any case) you do dig a well at the head of your field, release (it)!
(On account of the well which you dug) your feet (will be/are) strangers to your field,
To you, decreases (losses) are brought to you, much loss //
　　　and that which is yours they will remove/drag out of you by means of an oath.

12. Mistaken acquisitions and delusions to be avoided

Don't buy an ox in the spring (the season of grass); (cf. Šuruppak 217–21)
Don't take a maidservant in (the days) of a festi[val... (cf. Šuruppak 213)
The ox is go]od in the month of Sivan, the maidservant is dressed in festive garb,
(but) during the year good oil does not have interest, and is used for polishing.

13. Don't buy a spruced up (primping/masquerading) slave
who is not worth its price

Do not buy a refurbished? (primping/masquerading?) man/slave—
His price is half a mina of silver, (but) his true worth/price is only four silver.

14. Do not have consideration for a sad tenant

Do not make advice, as for the man, fix his lot! (other version: Do not make advice, fix the lot of the one who dwells with you)

And one who examines your insides, complete for him the heart (= be honest to
him?; other version: free for him the heart = speak freely)
And give him a month or two for punishment/fine.

15. Protect the family property and your secrets from legal adversity

Together with your brother, release the property of his hand (= which belongs to
him)!
His account (possessions), let not his rivals take away by lawsuit (cf. *BWL*, 102:76)
If the rival examines the chambers of your belly (*riqītaka*, cf. Prov 20:27
חופש כל חדרי בטן . . . it shall be opened.

16. Don't exchange the family home for a tent
(Summary and inclusio returning to opening topic)

[…] in connection to the life (of those who dwell in) tents, let me answer you—
[…] and your majesty
[in] your father's house they mention your name.
[…]… a man, the land without crowds of people
Our […]… his name, he dwells in an additional house
[…in] his sleep/dream he will cry
[…]… suitable for dwelling
[…] I will do well he will lay down
[…]…the lot (?) of his path
[…] he will cry
[…] in the house you will enter
[…] in the irrigated field
[…]…you shall lead away/lift up
you have repaired/strengthened the roof for the head and the foot, **my son!**
Have you built a house in order to stay awake at night?

The Son's Reply (cf. Psalm 49)

Introduction

The son opens his mouth // speaks and says to his father the counselor/king:
The word of my father the counselor/king I have heard // Now pay attention to me
and I will say something to you:

Man's nature is to be restless

We are doves, cooing birds //
(the human being) who wanders about most restlessly—of the strong ox, the bull of
heaven, the mighty bullock, we are his sons (cf. Ps 49:13, 15, 21).

Birth

Like a dam, Šamaš is the aide to the midwife.
The helper of Ištar is fire, which gives out payment to the midwives.

Work and its profits

My creditors/lenders do not swear "(I) own the principal."
Bailiff demons (*gallû*) watch over the plowing in the fields (and the garden) (in
order to know how much to take)."
Bread, made from plants, (the bailiff) does not eat // water in the irrigated field (the
bailiff?) does not drink.
The water, for which in order to drink he looks toward the heavens, do not
approach/flow (cf. Eccl 11:1–6).
[The…] he does [not?] wash/flood //
    and from the honored woman he does not bear (take) the tax.

Death and funeral and the father's inheritance

My Father! You have built a house; the door you have hung.
60 cubits (wide) is the warehouse, What have you taken? (cf. Ps 49:17–18; Eccl
2:18–21; 4:8–5:7)
The attic of your house is full of everything; (the room) alongside its warehouse is
full of grain (cf. Prov 24:3–4).
For the day of your fate (your death) 9 *Kor* are counted, and they are placed at your
head (cf. Prov 27:23–26).
In your possessions are thousands of ewes, a goat, fancy clothes, (they are) your portion alone.
All the property and the bread and the tax—the king, it's his money—will go out.

After death (cf. Eccl 9:10; Ps 49:12)

Many are the living beings which eat bread; many (are the living beings) who
become green (from want of) drink;
Many (of us) see the sun; many (of us) sit in the broad shadow (of the netherworld).

In the isolated house (or: ruin) people lie down—Ereškigal (goddess of the nether-world) is our mother, and we are her children.
"Shadows" (= dividers) are placed in the gate of the isolated house (or: the ruin) so that the living will not see the dead.

Colophon

This is the word/dispute/argument (*dabāba*) which the father and son aroused (*dekû*) together (cf. Prov 10:12).

PART THREE

Comparisons of Mesopotamian and Biblical Texts and Motifs

Sages with a Sense of Humor:
The Babylonian Dialogue between a Master and His Servant and the Book of Qohelet

Edward L. Greenstein

One of the most intriguing and amusing works of ancient Babylonian literature is the wisdom text known as the Dialogue between a Master and His Servant.[1] The text, which was apparently composed in the early first millennium B.C.E., was popular among Mesopotamian scribes. It has been found in five copies, although only one is relatively well preserved, and it seems to have circulated in two recensions, one Babylonian, one Assyrian. As its modern title indicates, the text presents a dialogue between a man and his man-servant, and it comprises ten or eleven stanzas, each of them devoted to a different topic. In each stanza the master summons his servant with the words "Servant, oblige me!"[2] and the servant answers, "Yes, my lord, yes!" The master discloses a plan he means to execute that day, and the servant offers immediate encouragement by providing a reason explaining why it is worthwhile to carry out the plan. But as soon as the master hears the servant's reply, he announces that he no longer intends to execute said plan: "No, my servant, I shall not do such and such." The servant greets the new decision with enthusiasm and finds a reason for which to commend it. Significantly, the servant is always given the last word.

Following about ten rounds of such hypothetical discussion, it finally dawns on the master that there is not a single activity that is worthwhile—neither traveling to

---

1. This study first appeared in Hebrew as an article in *Beth Mikra* 44 (1999): 97–106. It is reproduced here with only minor revisions and with the kind permission of the publisher. The article grew out of a lecture delivered at a symposium on satire and humor in the biblical world that took place at Haifa University, December 1997. I dedicate this publication of the article to the memory of Prof. Ze'ev Weisman of Haifa University. Translations of the texts are my own, unless otherwise noted. The standard edition of the Akkadian text is in *BWL*, 139–49. For a recent translation into English, see Benjamin R. Foster, *Before the Muses: An Anthology of Akkadian Literature* (2 vols.; 2nd ed.; Bethesda, Md.: CDL Press, 1996), 2.799–802.

2. For this sense of the verb *mitanguranni* (Gtn of *magāru*, "to be agreeable"), see E. A. Speiser, "The Case of the Obliging Servant," in *Oriental and Biblical Studies* (ed. J. J. Finkelstein and Moshe Greenberg; Philadelphia: University of Pennsylvania Press, 1967), 344–66, at 350–51. Foster translates: "Servant, listen to me" (*Before the Muses*).

the governor's palace nor giving his hands a ritual washing; neither going on a hunt nor building a family; neither engaging in crime nor loving a woman; neither sacrificing to a god nor making a loan, not even giving to charity. If so, the master asks his servant, "What is good?" "To break my neck and yours and to throw us into the river—that is good!" replies the brazen servant. "No, my servant, I will kill you and transport you (to the netherworld) ahead of me." "Then my master will not live three days after me."[3] With this exchange the dialogue ends.

The text treats a clearly philosophical issue—What is good?—and reaches the conclusion that none of the enterprises that engage humanity has any real value. For this reason Assyriologists once tended to the view that the dialogue was severe, and even pessimistic, in its outlook and tone, and they referred to the piece as the "Dialogue of Pessimism."[4] This assessment of the Babylonian text's bleakness was only reinforced by its comparison to the Bible's striking thematic parallel, the Book of Qohelet (Ecclesiastes), a Hebrew composition that has also been thought to be pervaded by a somber spirit.[5]

The comparison between the Babylonian Dialogue and Qohelet is certainly warranted.[6] Both the author of the Mesopotamian text and the author of Qohelet sug-

---

3. The idea seems to be either that the master, who appears in this text as entirely dependent on his servant for approval, will not be able to survive without him, or that on account of the brevity of life, the master will in any event live only a short time—"three days"—beyond the lifespan of his servant.

4. See, e.g., *BWL*, 139 n. 1. Cf. Wilfred G. Lambert, "Some New Babylonian Wisdom Literature," in *Wisdom in Ancient Israel: Essays in Honor of J. A. Emerton* (ed. John Day; Cambridge: Cambridge University Press, 1995), 30–42, esp. 36. For a survey of interpretations of the text, see Jean Bottéro, "The Dialogue of Pessimism and Transcendence," in *Mesopotamia: Writing, Reasoning, and the Gods* (trans. Z. Bahrani and M. Van De Mieroop; Chicago: University of Chicago Press, 1992), 251–76, esp. 257.

5. See, e.g., Bottéro, "The Dialogue of Pessimism," 260–61.

6. This is not the place to expatiate on the possible historical explanations for the clear and abundant textual parallels between the Babylonian Dialogue and the Book of Qohelet. There are actually quite specific parallels between Qohelet and Mesopotamian literature in general, and especially with the Epic of Gilgamesh; see below, n. 41. Let us content ourselves here with noting that Mesopotamian literature was an integral part of the education that Canaanite and early Israelite scribes received; see, e.g., Aaron Demsky, "The Education of Canaanite Scribes in the Mesopotamian Cuneiform Tradition," in *Bar-Ilan Studies in Assyriology Dedicated to Pinhas Artzi* (Ramat-Gan: Bar-Ilan University Press, 1990), 157–70. Syrian scribes in the mid-second millennium B.C.E. copied wisdom texts originating in Mesopotamia and even composed similar texts of their own; see, e.g., John Khanjian, "Wisdom in Ugarit and in the Ancient Near East with Particular Emphasis on Old Testament Wisdom Literature" (Ph.D. diss., Claremont Graduate School, 1974). One of the Akkadian wisdom texts found at Ugarit has been discovered at Emar as well; see Daniel Arnaud, *Emar IV/4* (Mission archéologique de Meskéné; Paris: Editions Recherche sur les Civilisations, 1987), 377–82. Another Mesopotamian text, resembling parts of the Gilgamesh Epic, has been found at both Ugarit and Emar; see Manfried Dietrich, "'Ein Leben ohne Freude . . .'; Studie über eine Weisheitkomposition aus den Gelehrtenbibliotheken von Emar und Ugarit," *UF* 24 (1992): 9–29. Compositions such as these attest to the wide dissemination of wisdom literature written in Akkadian in the land of Canaan and its environs in the Late Bronze Age. In light of the Mesopotamian background of wisdom literature in Canaan in the second millennium B.C.E., it is likely that Hebrew wisdom literature grew out of Canaanite roots and developed in ancient Israel under a sustained Mesopotamian influence. For aspects of wisdom in Ugaritic literature, see my study, "The Ugaritic Epic of Kirta in a Wisdom Perspective," *Te'uda* 16–17 (2001): 1–13 (in Hebrew).

gest reasons for doing one thing and reasons for doing its opposite (see further below). Like his Babylonian counterpart, Qohelet praises the dead and values them more than the living (Qoh 4:2). In Qohelet's estimation, "everything is mere breath" (הכל הבל),[7] and "what gain is there for the doer in the effort he makes?" (3:9). There are striking resemblances as well between the ways that the Babylonian and the Hebrew works treat the question of what is good—and bad—for a person. For example, the two texts berate women in a similar way. The servant in the Dialogue says, "woman is a snare, a snare, a pit, a ditch; / woman is a sharp iron sword that cuts a man's neck" (stanza 6).[8] Qohelet applies the same image to woman: "her heart is snares and traps, her arms are fetters; one who is pleasing to God will escape her, but a sinner will be captured by her" (7:26).

Furthermore, both sages characterize wisdom as being beyond a human's grasp. Qohelet relates, "I have tested all this through wisdom; I thought, 'I shall acquire wisdom' but it is remote from me; what goes on is remote, and deep, very deep—who can reach it?" (7:23–24).[9] Toward the end of the Babylonian Dialogue, the servant seems to quote a similar Mesopotamian proverb: "Who is so tall as to ascend the heavens? / Who is so broad as to encompass the netherworld?"[10] It is also clear that both sages, the Babylonian and the Hebrew, are disturbed by the fact that the righteous and the wicked are allotted the same fate, with no differentiation in accordance with their behavior; the regrettable conclusion is that there is no justice. Qohelet, for example, asserts, "There is a worthless thing (הבל) that is done on earth, whereby righteous people receive their due according to the behavior of the wicked, and there are wicked people who receive their due according to the behavior of the righteous; I say, this too is worthless (הבל)" (8:14). In the same vein, the servant in the Dialogue avers that if his master would go walking "upon the ancient tells" and contemplate "the skulls of the earlier and later ones," he would not be able to discern "which is the evildoer and which the doer of good" (end of stanza 9).

In addition to these parallels, we may remark that both characters in search of what is good, Qohelet and the Babylonian master, are aristocrats who enjoy the leisure

---

7. The term הבל, which has the basic meaning of "vapor, breath," conveys a sense of the ephemeral and insubstantial. In the scheme of Qohelet's thought, things that do not last have no real value, so that הבל can by extension denote things of no worth. Michael Fox is surely correct that Qohelet uses the term הבל to characterize situations that he finds to be "absurd," but I do not agree that this is the meaning of the term, only one of its applications. See Michael V. Fox, "The Meaning of *hebel* for Qohelet," *JBL* 105 (1986): 409–27.

8. The reference to cutting the neck is probably a proto-Freudian reference to castration; see my discussion in "Some Developments in the Study of Language and Some Implications for the Study of Ancient Languages and Cultures," in *Semitic Linguistics: The State of the Art at the Turn of the Twenty-First Century* (ed. Shlomo Izre'el; IOS 20; Winona Lake, Ind.: Eisenbrauns, 2002), 441–79, at 458.

9. For "deep" as a quality of esoteric wisdom, see my article, "The Poem on Wisdom in Job 28 in Its Conceptual and Literary Contexts," in *Job 28: Cognition in Context* (ed. Ellen van Wolde; Leiden: Brill, 2003), 253–80.

10. For the proverb, its forms, and its history, see Frederick E. Greenspahn, "A Mesopotamian Proverb and Its Biblical Reverberations," *JAOS* 114 (1994): 33–38.

to engage in an impractical philosophical endeavor. Neither seems to need to make a living.[11] Like the master in the Dialogue, Qohelet is able to try out any activity under the sun that interests him.

Even the form of the dialogue, which obviously defines the entire Babylonian text, is not alien to Qohelet. While it is true that Qohelet has no conversational partner, as the Babylonian master does, he does have a different though analogous interlocutor—his heart: "I spoke with my heart" (1:16); "I said in my heart" (2:1; 3:17); "I set my heart to seek and explore wisdom" (1:13); "I set my heart to know wisdom" (1:17); and so forth. The Babylonian sage casts his ideas in the form of a dialogue between two parties, while the Hebrew sage casts his ideas in the form of a report on what transpires between the speaker and his heart. We may finally note a stylistic parallel as well. Compare, for example, the contrastive presentation in the catalogue of times for activities and their opposites in Qohelet 3—"a time to give birth and a time to die," "a time to plant and a time to uproot the planted," etc.—to the way the servant expresses himself in the Babylonian Dialogue: "to hunger and [then] to eat, to thirst and (then) to drink, that is the way it goes for a man" (stanza 2).

The affinity of Qohelet to the Dialogue between a Master and His Servant is manifest overall. The scholarly view that the Dialogue is a pessimistic, depressing text is influenced in part, as was said, by its comparison to Qohelet, which reflects, in the prevailing opinion, a pessimistic and even tragic outlook.[12]

The notion that the Dialogue takes a thoroughly somber perspective began to change with the argument of E. A. Speiser that the text contains humorous elements.[13] Speiser does not deny the seriousness of purpose in the Dialogue's thought, but he maintains that the tone in which that purpose is articulated is fairly lighthearted. In building his argument, Speiser indicates several features of the text that do not comport with the pessimistic attitude that is attributed to it. First, he reminds us that alongside every pessimistic utterance of the servant is an optimistic one. For example:

"Servant, oblige me!" "Yes, master, yes."
"Hurry, ready and hitch up my chariot so that I may travel to the wilds!"
"Travel, master, travel! The belly of the wanderer is always full.
"The scavenging dog splinters a bone;
"The wandering raven builds a nest.
"The skipping onager eats its fill of grass."
"No, my servant, to the wilds I will not travel."
"Do not travel, master, do not travel!"
"The wanderer goes out of his mind.

---

11. So Bottéro, "The Dialogue of Pessimism," 257.

12. See, e.g., Michael V. Fox, *Qohelet and His Contradictions* (Sheffield: Almond Press, 1989), esp. 33; James L. Crenshaw, "Qoheleth in Current Research," in *Urgent Advice and Probing Questions: Collected Writings on Old Testament Wisdom* (Macon, Ga.: Mercer University Press, 1995), 522.

13. Speiser, "The Case of the Obliging Servant."

"The scavenging dog breaks his teeth.

"The wandering raven nests in a wall.

"The skipping onager—his home is the wilderness" (stanza 3).

In sum, there are reasons to go hunting, and there are reasons not to go.

Second, Speiser observes that the servant does not necessarily express his personal opinions. His function is to recommend every plan his master proposes. Accordingly, when the servant furnishes a justification for his master's proposal, he often formulates his advice by way of a traditional saying or proverb. For example, in response to the master's proposal to wash his hands and dine, the servant replies: "The god Shamash accompanies hands that are (ritually) washed" (stanza 2). And in response to the master's plan to loan money, the servant replies: "To give is like loving a woman, but to return is like childbirth!" (stanza 8).

Speiser suggests as well that the text's attitude toward the gods is derisive, at least if one takes the words at their face value. When the master cancels his decision to make a sacrifice to his personal god, the servant seconds the new proposal with the following, somewhat outrageous, remark: "Do not, my master, do not! / Teach your god to follow you like a dog, / Whether he makes a cultic demand of you or whether (he asks of you), 'Make inquiry of your god!'" (stanza 7). In other words, do not bother to take instruction from your god; train him to follow after you.

It appears likely to Speiser that such extreme language does not bespeak a deadly serious text, a text devoid of humor. To the contrary, the text's ridicule of the gods goes hand in glove with its pervasive display of ridicule toward the master and the upper class he represents. The ridicule finds expression in the character of the clever and brazen servant. His relation toward the divine sphere and the sociopolitical one is satirical. As the Assyriologist Jean Bottéro has indicated, however, the satirical humor in the Dialogue does not detract from its serious philosophical import.[14]

I not only share the view that the Babylonian text is essentially satirical; I believe that one can find other sorts of humor in it as well. A satirical text need not produce laughter, but I think it is funny. In Henri Bergson's well-known theory of humor, people appear comical when they refuse to alter their behavior even as circumstances change. When something happens, to them or in their surroundings, they seem to react mechanically.[15] In the Dialogue, both characters behave in predictable form. The master proposes a plan and will immediately replace it with an opposite one. The compliant servant supports and justifies his master's proposals. The formulaic opening of each and every stanza is the quintessence of the overall pattern: the master calls on his servant, and the servant indicates his readiness. The conduct of the master and the servant is, in Bergson's terms, comical.

---

14. Bottéro, "The Dialogue of Pessimism," 260.

15. Henri Bergson, "Laughter," in *Comedy* (ed. Wylie Sypher; Baltimore: Johns Hopkins University Press, 1956), 61–190. Simon Critchley suggests an alternative explanation: people are humorous when they behave in an unhuman manner, which includes, in particular, animal-like behavior; see Simon Critchley, *On Humour* (London and New York: Routledge, 2002).

According to most theories, what produces humor is the sudden discovery of incongruence between two things. As Sigmund Freud explains it, in his famous monograph on wit, the incongruence is discerned when we observe certain resemblances between two things that are supposed to be different.[16] For example, a monkey dressed like a man.[17] Actually, a monkey looks and behaves a lot like a man, and vice versa. If so, why not dress a monkey in human attire? However, it is not a sufficient cause of humor to recognize the similar within the different. Freud lays stress on another prerequisite of humor, and that is economy of expression and rapidity of perception.[18] The discord must be perceived without hesitation; a joke must be understood at once. It is therefore funny to hear the servant advise his master that a person should train his god like a puppy dog. The incongruence can be immediately grasped because it is formulated with concision: "like a dog." When one analyzes a joke, or reflects on it, as I am doing here, it completely kills the humor.

The servant's formulation is humorous because you cannot literally train your god. A god is not a dog. The dog is meant to be subordinate to the human, just as the human is meant to be subservient to the god (and a servant is meant to be beholden to his master). Yet a certain truth is captured in the utterance: someone who fulfills a god's demands expects to receive divine dividends, so that it seems that the god is dependent on the cultic offerings of the devotee.[19] Let us recall the Babylonian flood story as it is retold in the Epic of Gilgamesh. Following the period of the flood, during which no offerings could be made to the gods, the gods descend like flies upon the sacrifice of thanksgiving that was made by the hero Utnapishtim.[20] The depiction of hungry deities, in need of food just like flies, is no less satirical than the comparison of gods and dogs made by the servant in the Dialogue.[21]

The Dialogue's humor tends to be conveyed rapidly.[22] The master proposes his current plan in the form a single sentence, and the servant approves it at once. The vacillations in the master's decision making are likewise expressed economically in a single sentence, and the servant, as usual, takes no time in providing a reason in support of the alternate plan. As was said, both reasons—to do and not to do—flow out of the reservoir of received wisdom.[23] The satirical sting in the text strikes right at wis-

---

16. Sigmund Freud, "Wit and Its Relation to the Unconscious," in *The Basic Writings of Sigmund Freud* (ed. A. A. Brill; New York: Modern Library, 1938), 631–803, esp. 634.

17. Critchley would rather explain this as exposure of a human's animal side (*On Humour*).

18. Freud, "Wit and Its Relation to the Unconscious," 654. See also John A. Paulos, *Mathematics and Humor: A Study of the Logic of Humor* (Chicago: University of Chicago Press, 1980).

19. And anyone who has owned a dog will know how a human is often subject to its dictates.

20. Gilgamesh XI, lines 160–62 in the edition of Simo Parpola, *The Standard Babylonian Epic of Gilgamesh* (State Archives of Assyria Cuneiform Texts 1; Helsinki: University of Helsinki, 1997); lines 164–66 in the translation of Benjamin R. Foster, *The Epic of Gilgamesh* (New York: W. W. Norton, 2001), 90.

21. See, e.g., Helmer Ringgren, *Religions of the Ancient Near East* (trans. James Sturdy; Philadelphia: Westminster, 1973), 72.

22. Several rhetorical strategies in the Dialogue were pointed out in a paper by my former student Varda Bergman.

23. See, e.g., Bottéro, "The Dialogue of Pessimism," 259.

dom itself, which is characterized here as a compendium of contrary counsel, of contradictory advice. Wisdom, according to the Dialogue, advises one thing and its opposite, and the ineluctable conclusion is to do nothing. This is exactly what happens in the comical high-brow drama of the master and servant: they speak much and do nothing. Anyone who wishes to follow this wisdom will refrain from all activity.

The Book of Qohelet abounds in inconsistency.[24] Commentators count between twenty and thirty contradictions. The problem of internal contradictions in Qohelet has been addressed in a famous pericope in the Babylonian Talmud (*b. Šabb.* 30b):

> The sages sought to suppress the Book of Qohelet because its statements contradict one another.... What is the basis of the assertion that its statements contradict one another? It is written "Better is anger than laughter" (7:3) and it is written "To laughter I said: Praiseworthy!" (2:2). It is written "So I lauded levity" (8:15) and it is written "As for levity, what can it do?" (2:2).

A book of philosophy that contradicts itself did not make sense to the classical rabbis, as R. Abraham Ibn Ezra explains in his commentary on Qoh 7:3: "It is well known that even the merest of thinkers will not compose a book in which he contradicts himself." The rabbis therefore resolved the contradictions by assigning a different context to each apparently contradictory proposition:

> There is no contradiction. "Better is anger than laughter" means: better is the anger of the Holy One Blessed Be He on the righteous in the present world than the laughter of the Holy One Blessed Be He on the wicked in the world to come! "And to laughter I said: Praiseworthy!"—this is the laughter of the Holy One Blessed Be He with the righteous in the present world. "So I lauded levity"—the levity involved in performing a mitzvah. "And as for levity, what can it do?"—this is levity that is not involved in performing a mitzvah.

Ibn Ezra took a similar approach by suggesting a different set of circumstances surrounding each seemingly disparate statement.[25] R. Samuel ben Meir was also disturbed by the apparent contradictions in Qohelet and tried to resolve them by way of creative philology. For example, he interpreted *měhôlāl* in the phrase "To laughter I said: Praiseworthy! (*měhôlāl*)" not in the ordinary sense of *h-l-l*, "praise," but rather in relation to *hôlēlût*, "frivolity," in Qoh 1:17 (commentary to 2:2).[26] Some scholars in our day explain the contradictions by the theory that in each pair of discordant propo-

---

24. See Mordechai Zer-Kavod, "Introduction" to Qohelet, in *The Five Scrolls* (Da'at Miqra'; Jerusalem: Mossad Ha-Rav Kook, 1973), 24–33 (Hebrew); Fox, *Qohelet and His Contradictions*, 11–15, 19–28.

25. For a discussion of Ibn Ezra's approach to the contradictions in Qohelet, see Zer-Kavod, "Introduction," 26–27.

26. Sara Japhet and Robert B. Salters, *The Commentary of R. Samuel Ben Meir on* Qoheleth (Jerusalem: Magnes Press, 1985), 63–68. H. L. Ginsberg had interpreted similarly; see H. L. Ginsberg, *Studies in Koheleth* (New York: Jewish Theological Seminary, 1950), 2; but he abandoned this interpretation in his later commentary; idem, *Qohelet* (Tel Aviv and Jerusalem: M. Neumann, 1961), 66 (Hebrew).

sitions, one is being cited from another source and one belongs to Qohelet.[27] However, there is no text-linguistic basis to the identification of the alleged quotations, nor is there any way of telling which statement belongs to the putative source and which to Qohelet.[28]

I am more inclined to the approach of Michael Fox, who allows the discordant utterances to stand side by side without harmonization.[29] Contradiction and irony are an integral and natural part of existence and they cannot be resolved. It's a topsy turvy world. This is what leads to the notion that everything is "worthless" (הבל), which Fox interprets as "absurd."[30] Fox holds, however, that there is no humor in the irony that characterizes Qohelet.[31] The situation is not funny, it is tragic. Fox maintains that the Babylonian Dialogue as well depicts a world that is by nature absurd.[32]

As regards the main lines of the outlook that is shared by Qohelet and the Babylonian Dialogue, I am in agreement with Fox. And like him, I do not find in Qohelet the same comical strain that typifies the Dialogue. However, I do not think that Qohelet is devoid of humor. I maintain that one can discern in Qohelet a number of humorous elements. In this I follow Edwin Good, who underscores the ironic perspective that pervades the book and goes so far as to interpret the term הבל as incongruence, as irony.[33]

The comical character of the fool (סכל, כסיל) in Qohelet has been treated at some length by Etan Levine,[34] and the satirical political anecdotes in the book have been discussed by Ze'ev Weisman.[35] There are well-known examples of wordplay—a feature that is humorous at root but not necessarily funny. An example is Qoh 7:6: "For the laughter (śĕḥôq) of the fool (kĕsîl) is like the sound of nettles (sîrîm) under a pot (sîr)." The word sîr can refer to both a nettle and a cooking pot.[36] The repetitive sound of sibilants in the words sîr and sîrîm, as well as in śĕḥôq and kĕsîl, onomatopoeically imitates the crackling of the burning nettles.[37]

---

27. E.g., Robert Gordis, *Koheleth: The Man and His World* (New York: Schocken Books, 1968), 95–108; J. A. Loader, *Polar Structures in the Book of Qohelet* (Berlin: de Gruyter, 1979), 20–21. For a survey of scholarship dealing with the problem of contradictions in Qohelet, see Crenshaw, "Qoheleth in Current Research," 522–29.

28. Fox, *Qohelet and His Contradictions*, 27–28.

29. Ibid.

30. See above, n. 7.

31. Fox, *Qohelet and His Contradictions*, 33.

32. Ibid., 32–33.

33. Edwin M. Good, *Irony in the Old Testament* (Philadelphia: Westminster Press, 1965), 176–83.

34. Etan Levine, "Qoheleth's Fool: A Composite Portrait," in *On Humour and the Comic in the Hebrew Bible* (ed. Yehuda T. Radday and Athalya Brenner; Sheffield: Almond Press, 1990), 277–94.

35. Ze'ev Weisman, *Political Satire in the Bible* (Jerusalem: Mossad Bialik, 1996), 221–34 (Hebrew). (This section is not reproduced in the 1998 English edition of the book.)

36. See, e.g., David Yellin, "לתורת המליצה התנכית," [On Biblical Rhetoric], *Selected Writings* (2 vols.; Jerusalem: David Yellin Jubilee Committee, 1939), 2:86–87.

37. See, e.g., Meir Weiss, *The Bible from Within: The Method of Total Interpretation* (Jerusalem: Magnes Press, 1984), 131.

In light of the humorous character of the Babylonian Dialogue, in which we find a string of contradictory propositions as one plan is supplanted by its opposite, we may also find the reversals in the Book of Qohelet to be humorous, wherever they appear in relatively rapid succession. That is, a contradiction may take on a humorous aspect when it occurs in close proximity to the proposition it contradicts. Sudden turnabouts, like the ups and downs of a roller-coaster ride, produce the entertaining effect.

We encounter a sudden change of direction of this sort in a statement such as we find in Qoh 2:3: "And while my heart conducts itself with wisdom, to take hold of folly."[38] A comparison with 2:12 makes it clear that "folly" (סכלות) is synonymous with "frivolity" (הוללות). The juxtaposition of "conducting oneself with wisdom" and "to take hold of folly" is rather paradoxical, and the formulation of the phrases in brief utterances with only the conjunctive *waw* between them is minimalist. The similarities in the syntax of the two phrases (verb–preposition ב–noun), together with their equivalent prosodic length, produce a parallelism between them. Parallelism in form creates the expectation that the parallel parts will have some semantic relation between them.[39] It therefore causes us no little surprise when we realize that in this juxtaposition we are holding not two ends of the same rope but two altogether different ones.

Consider as well Qoh 4:6: "Better is a handful of satisfaction than two fistfuls of striving (עמל) and pursuit of wind." The reader of this verse may puzzle over what is said just six verses further on: "Two are better than one, when they have some good in their efforts/profits (עמל)" (4:12). First, the former verse informs us that two are not always better than one. One handful of satisfaction is preferable to two of strain. Moreover, the former verse suggests that it is advisable to stay far from עמל, while the latter verse asserts that it is good for two to engage in עמל together. There would seem to be a bit of humor in this puzzlement.[40]

In a similar fashion, the sage asserts in 7:3 that "better is anger than laughter," while only six verses later he advises, "Do not allow your spirit to hasten to anger" (7:9). True, the situations in the two instances may be different. It is better to be angry than to be frivolous, yet better never to come to anger at all. Even so, the juxtaposition of positive and negative propositions about anger may suffice to prompt a humorous response.

---

38. For נהג in the sense of "conducting oneself," see, e.g., James L. Crenshaw, *Ecclesiastes: A Commentary* (OTL; Philadelphia: Westminster Press, 1987), 78. In Ginsberg's emendation of the verse, the juxtaposition is even more striking: "I set forth to draw [...] on wisdom and to take hold of frivolity"; see Ginsberg, *Qohelet*, 67.

39. See Edward L. Greenstein, "How Does Parallelism Mean?" in *A Sense of Text* (JQRSupp 1982; Winona Lake, Ind.: Eisenbrauns, 1983), 41–70, at 64.

40. C. L. Seow points to contradictions of this kind when he remarks that the series of "better than . . ." (. . . מ טוב) sayings in Qoh 4:1–16 follows on the heels of chap. 3, where it is asserted that there is no good for a person except to enjoy what one earns or receives (see 3:12, 22). Similarly, Seow points out the same sort of contradiction between Qoh 6:11 ("Who knows what is good for a person . . .") and 7:1–12, another series of "better than . . ." sayings, in each of which one of the two things that are compared is regarded as "good" (טוב). See Choon-Leong Seow, *Ecclesiastes* (AB; Garden City, N.Y.: Doubleday, 1997), 186.

Qohelet, like the Babylonian Dialogue, pits traditional but contrary sayings one against the other. Qohelet, too, would seem to draw its epigrams from ancient sources.[41] Let us take as an example Qoh 9:4: "For it is better for a live dog than a dead lion."[42] The proposition seems true, as the sage explains in what follows. But it can hardly be reconciled with a saying found in 6:3: "Better than him (viz., who leaves his worldly goods to another) is the stillborn." In other words, it is better for one who has never lived than for someone who lives a normal existence in this world. According to this statement, it is better to be dead than alive, whether we are speaking of a person, a dog, or a lion.[43] That, however, is not the ultimate point. The ultimate idea is this: whoever relies on traditional wisdom will inevitably discover that its sayings contradict one another. Wisdom cannot serve as a guide to life because it is self-contradictory and can lead to divergent and even contrary conclusions.

Qohelet never refers to wisdom itself as "worthless" (הבל). After all, "there is an advantage to wisdom over folly, like the advantage of light over darkness; the wise person has eyes in his head, while the fool goes in darkness" (2:13–14). Nevertheless, wisdom does not have an absolute value. Qohelet's criticism of wisdom is not direct but indirect, by way of a satirical approach toward received wisdom. For every cogent statement there is an equally compelling counterstatement. Lest we understand him in an overly literal and serious manner, he reminds us of his light-hearted outlook through his use of hyperbole, as, for example, in 6:6: "Even were he to live a thousand years, twice, and were never to experience any pleasure..."; or through comical images, as, for example, in 5:11: "Sweet is the sleep of the worker, whether he eats little or

---

41. On Qohelet's apparent use of a passage best known from the Epic of Gilgamesh X, see, e.g., H. L. Ginsberg, "The Quintessence of Koheleth," in *Biblical and Other Studies* (ed. Alexander Altmann; Cambridge, Mass.: Harvard University Press, 1963), 58–59; Jean de Savignac, "La sagesse du Qohéleth et l'épopée de Gilgamesh," *VT* 28 (1978): 318–23. Since 1905 scholars have pointed out additional parallels between Qohelet and the Gilgamesh Epic; e.g., Qoh 4:9–12 and the Sumerian text Gilgamesh and the Land of the Living, lines 106–10; see Samuel N. Kramer, "Gilgamesh and the Land of the Living," *JCS* 1 (1947): 3–46; Qoh 5:15 and the Old Babylonian version of the Gilgamesh Epic, IV, line 15; see Aaron Schafer, "The Mesopotamian Background of Qohelet 4:9–12," *Eretz-Israel* 8 (E. L. Sukenik volume; Jerusalem: Israel Exploration Society, 1967): 246–50 (Hebrew); idem, "New Information on the Source of 'the Three-fold Cord,'" *Eretz-Israel* 9 (W. F. Albright volume; Jerusalem: Israel Exploration Society, 1969): 159–60 (Hebrew). And see, in general, Bruce W. Jones, "From Gilgamesh to Qoheleth," in *Scripture in Context III: The Bible in the Light of Cuneiform Literature* (ed. William W. Hallo et al.; Lewiston, N.Y.: Edwin Mellen Press, 1990), 349–79. For a parallel between Qohelet as an autobiographical text and the Mesopotamian "Cuthean Legend," see Tremper Longman III, *Fictional Akkadian Autobiography: A Generic and Comparative Study* (Winona Lake, Ind.: Eisenbrauns, 1991), 120–23.

42. Cf. R. B. Y. Scott, *Proverbs, Ecclesiastes* (AB; Garden City, N.Y.: Doubleday, 1965), 246. For the preposition ל preceding the word כלב, "dog," in an emphatic function, in the sense of "indeed," see Seow, *Ecclesiastes*, 301.

43. The contradiction leads traditional commentators and some contemporary scholars to interpret the saying about the live dog ironically; e.g., Ibn Ezra ad loc.; James L. Crenshaw, "The Shadow of Death in Qoheleth," in *Urgent Advice and Probing Questions*, 580–81.

much, while the satiety of the wealthy does not allow him to sleep at all!" The world-view of Qohelet is cynical, yes, and even depressing; but it is not without its humor.

Near the beginning of his quest for what is good, Qohelet remarks: "Moreover, my wisdom sustained (lit., stood by) me" (2:9). If we succeed in discerning the humorous elements in the book, we may come to feel that his sense of humor has sustained him as well.

Cosmos, Temple, House:
Building and Wisdom
in Mesopotamia and Israel

Raymond C. Van Leeuwen

For Baruch A. Levine

1. Ancient Mesopotamian Pictures of Building and Creation[1]

The present essay considers the importance of "house building" for understanding lived reality and cognitive environments in Israel and Mesopotamia. Through the comparison of ancient building accounts and their biblical counterparts, I argue that both Mesopotamians and Israelites saw wise human house building and other cultural activities as rooted in the divine wisdom of creation. Both Mesopotamians and Israelites grounded human wisdom in the divine wisdom, which gave order, meaning, and life to the cosmos as a whole.[2] Creation was portrayed as a macrocosmic "house"—with its fields, waters, and variegated activities—to which temples and ordinary houses with their lands corresponded as microcosms: "At home the more important gods were simply manorial lords administering their great temple estates, seeing

---

1. My sincere thanks to Peter Machinist, Mark S. Smith, and Kenton Sparks for helpful comments on an earlier draft of this essay, and to Richard Clifford for his labors on the manuscript. Responsibility for any remaining shortcomings belongs to me and perhaps Bill Gates.

2. Of the basic metaphors for cosmic creation (biological, conflictual, magical, or technical), Egypt's were primarily biological, while Israel's were primarily technical ("artifizialistisch"). So Othmar Keel, "Altägyptische und biblische Weltbilder, die Anfänge der vorsokratischen Philosophie und das ἀρχή-Problem in späten biblischen Schriften," in *Das biblische Weltbild und seine altorientalischen Kontexte* (ed. Bernd Janowski and Beate Ego; FAT 32; Tübingen: Mohr Siebeck, 2001), 34–36, 46–47. On the pre-Socratic use of architecture for cosmological reflection, see especially Robert Hahn, *Anaximander and the Architects: The Contributions of Egyptian and Greek Architectural Technologies to the Origins of Greek Philosophy* (Albany: State University of New York, 2001). Hahn, however, does not explore the ancient Near Eastern background concerning Greek building, craft, and cosmology. Among recent works, see Sarah P. Morris, *Daidalos and the Origins of Greek Art* (Princeton: Princeton University Press, 1992); and Martin L. West, *The East Face of Helicon: West Asiatic Elements in Greek Poetry and Myth* (Oxford: Clarendon Press, 1997).

to it that plowing, sowing, and reaping were done at the right times, and keeping order in the towns and villages that belonged to the manor."[3]

My particular focus is the widespread pattern of "house building" and "house filling," or provision, as it combines with the topos of the builder's wisdom. The language of "filling" (*malû*) refers first to the furnishings and inhabitants of a house, and, second, to all that makes life in the house abundant and rich, including agriculture, fertility, food and drink, and the acquisition of material goods.[4] This later aspect of filling I call provisioning, in which *water* supply and land management are crucial.

In English, terms like "building," and "creation" may refer either to a *process* or to the *result* of that process. In terms of the ancient topos described below, ordinary building and creation as building both entail a binary *process*: (1) of design, gathering materials and workers, construction, and completion; and (2) of filling the house with fitting contents and subsequently provisioning it.

As a *result* of that double process, one finds a house filled and provisioned with good things from the gardens, fields, and broader world outside, a place to celebrate with abundance.

My approach agrees with recent scholarship that argues that the ancient Near Eastern "house of the father" functioned materially and culturally to organize the life world of ancient societies.[5] For all their specific differences, Mesopotamian and Levantine societies not only organized their material world as house(hold)s but also developed cognitive environments in which this metaphoric domain or symbol expressed their particular understandings of the cosmo-social order comprising god(s) and humans.[6] For Assyrians to speak of "the house of Omri" (*Bît-Humria*)[7] or Arameans

---

3. Thorkild Jacobsen, *The Treasures of Darkness: A History of Mesopotamian Religion* (New Haven: Yale University Press, 1976), 81.

4. See Manfried Dietrich, "Der 'Garten Eden' und die babylonischen Parkanlagen im Tempelbezirk," in *Religiöse Landschaften* (ed. Johannes Hahn and Ronning Christian; AOAT 301; Münster: Ugarit Verlag, 2002), 1–29; Stephen W. Holloway, "What Ship Goes There: The Flood Narratives in the Gilgamesh Epic and Genesis Considered in Light of Ancient Near Eastern Temple Ideology," *ZAW* 103 (1991): 336–37; Donald J. Wiseman, "Palace and Temple Gardens in the Ancient Near East," in *Monarchies and Socio-Religious Traditions in the Ancient Near East* (ed. Takahito Mikasa; Wiesbaden: Harrassowitz, 1984), 37–43. On the limitations of the architectural evidence, see Amélie Kuhrt, "The Palace(s) of Babylon," in *The Royal Palace Institution in the First Millennium BC: Regional Development and Cultural Interchange Between East and West* (ed. Inge Nielsen; MDAI 4; Copenhagen: Danish Institute at Athens, 2001), 77–93.

5. J. David Schloen, *The House of the Father as Fact and Symbol: Patrimonialism in Ugarit and the Ancient Near East* (Studies in the Archaeology and History of the Levant; Winona Lake, Ind.: Eisenbrauns, 2001). See also Mark S. Smith, *The Origins of Biblical Monotheism: Israel's Polytheistic Background and the Ugaritic Texts* (New York: Oxford University Press, 2001), 54–66; Baruch A. Levine, "The Clan-Based Economy of Biblical Israel," in *Symbiosis, Symbolism, and the Power of the Past: Canaan, Ancient Israel, and Their Neighbors from the Late Bronze Age Through Roman Palaestina* (ed. William G. Dever and Seymour Gitin; Winona Lake, Ind.: Eisenbrauns, 2003), 445–53; Lawrence E. Stager, "The Patrimonial Kingdom of Solomon," in *Symbiosis*, 63–74; and from a different perspective, Shlomo Bunimovitz and Avraham Faust, "Building Identity: The Four-Room House and the Israelite Mind," *Symbiosis*, 411–23.

6. Schloen, *House of the Father*, 51.

7. *ARAB* 1.815, 816; Tiglath-pileser III. Text in Hayim Tadmor, *The Inscriptions of Tiglath-Pileser III, King of Assyria* (Jerusalem: Israel Academy of Sciences and Humanities, 1994), 140–41, 186–89, 202–3.

of "the house of David" (*byt dwd*)[8] was to use an expression and mode of thought common throughout the ancient Near East.[9]

As so often, Sumerian traditions are foundational for later developments.[10] An early hymn from the late third millennium may serve to introduce our enquiry. In the Sumerian text, "Enki and the World Order," Enki, the god of wisdom, engages in self-praise, much like that of Lady Wisdom in Proverbs 8.[11]

> In a state of high delight Enki, the king of the Abzu, again justly praises himself in his majesty: "I am the lord, I am one whose word is reliable, I am one who excels in everything.
>
> "At my command, sheepfolds have been built, cow-pens have been fenced off. When I approach heaven, a rain of abundance rains from heaven. When I approach earth, there is a high carp-flood. When I approach the green meadows, at my word stockpiles and stacks are accumulated. I have built my house, a shrine, in a pure place, and named it with a good name. I have built my Abzu, a shrine, in ......, and decreed a good fate for it. The shade of my house extends over the ...... pool. By my house the *suḫur* carp dart among the honey plants, and the *eštub* carp wave their tails among the small *gizi* reeds. The small birds chirp in their nests."[12]

Enki speaks of building his "house," but this term appears to cover several realms, which we may describe in terms of concentric, interactive circles, utilizing the ancient pattern of micro- and macrocosmos. Each house is like one in a series of Russian babushka dolls, in which each smaller doll nests inside the next larger. Most locally, the "house" is Enki's literal temple in Eridu, which he "builds" with the agency of human workers. Next in scope, the "house" is the chthonic sweet waters, or Abzu, the source of all wisdom, the cosmic domain of Enki,[13] whose waters fructify the earth. Finally, Enki's "house" is the entire cosmos, which is made prosperous from out of the local temple/Abzu with its gifts of life-giving waters. Enki/Ea is generally identi-

---

8. From the large literature, see William M. Schniedewind, "Tel Dan Stele: New Light on Aramaic and Jehu's Revolt," *BASOR* 302 (1996): 75–90; Paul-E. Dion, "The Tel Dan Stele and Its Historical Significance," in *Historical, Epigraphical and Biblical Studies in Honor of Professor Michael Heltzer* (ed. Yitzhak Avishur and Robert Deutsch; Tel Aviv and Jaffa: Archeological Center, 1999), 145–56.

9. See Schloen, *House of the Father*, 255–316; for the Old Babylonian period, Dominique Charpin in Charpin, Dietz Otto Edzard, and Marten Stol, *Mesopotamien: Die altbabylonische Zeit* (OBO 160/4; Göttingen: Vandenhoeck & Ruprecht, 2004), 232–316, especially 249–51.

10. Richard E. Averbeck, "Sumer, the Bible, and Comparative Method: Historiography and Temple Building," in *Mesopotamia and the Bible: Comparative Explorations* (ed. Mark W. Chavalas and K. Lawson Younger; JSOTSup 341; London: Sheffield Academic Press, 2002), 88–125.

11. See Samuel N. Kramer and John Maier, *Myths of Enki, the Crafty God* (New York: Oxford University Press, 1989), 38–56.

12. "Enki and the World Order," lines 86–99. Text from "The Electronic Text Corpus of Sumerian Literature" (ETCSL), available online at http://etcsl.orinst.ox.ac.uk/cgi-bin/etcsl.cgi?text=t.1.1.3#.

13. Wayne Horowitz, *Mesopotamian Cosmic Geography* (Mesopotamian Civilizations; Winona Lake, Ind.: Eisenbrauns, 1998), 17–18, 306–17, 334–47.

fied in ancient Near East iconography by the waters flowing from his shoulders or about his temple.[14]

Several matters here require mention. First, there is an easy symbolic interaction of house as dwelling place (É.GAL, or "big house") and as cosmic realm.[15] Second, we have a two-step process involving (a) the building of a "house" and (b) its provisioning or filling. Indeed, as wise organizer of the cosmos, Enki performs this function also for the other gods and their temples. A recurrent refrain in "Enki and the World Order" is "The Ekur, the house of Enlil, he [Enki] packed with goods" (e.g., lines 367–68). Much of the poem describes the fertility and universal well-being that Enki's waters and wisdom bring. This traditional thought picture lasted many centuries. At his ascension to the throne, Assurbanipal claims that "Adad let loose the rains and Ea [=Enki] released the (underground) springs," so that his reign was a period of surpassing abundance.[16] Third, the means by which Enki's house brings life, prosperity, and fertility to fill the earth are the waters above and below, just as in Prov 3:19–20 (see below).

In Israel also, water was often associated with wisdom: "The teaching of a wise man [masc. sing.] is a fountain of life . . ." (Prov 13:14a). "The words of one's mouth are deep waters, a flowing stream, a fountain of wisdom" (Prov 18:4). Moreover, the wife, who throughout Proverbs is a symbol of wisdom, is pictured in metaphors of life-giving water (5:15–20). But divine wisdom in Israel especially concerned the *organization* of water distribution and the limits placed on chaotic waters. This is a fundamental presupposition of YHWH's wisdom in Psalm 104. Only a few examples of this well-known theme are possible here: "Who shut in the sea with doors . . . and imposed my boundary on it (ואשבר עליו חקי),[17] and set bars and doors, and said, 'Thus far shall you come and no farther, and here shall your proud waves be stayed'?" (Job 38:8a, 10–11; cf. Pss 65:9–13 [Heb. 10–14]; 104 *passim*; Jer 5:22; Prov 8:24, 27–29; Qoh 2:5–6). Mesopotamian tradition speaks similarly of "the bolt, the bar of the sea" which is given in Enki's care to keep the waters in place within the cosmic house.[18]

---

14. Dominique Collon, *First Impressions: Cylinder Seals in the Ancient Near East* (Chicago: University of Chicago Press, 1988), nos. 760–62, 847–48, 672–73.

15. For the widespread homology of cosmos, house, and body, see Mircea Eliade, *The Myth of the Eternal Return or, Cosmos and History* (trans. Willard R. Trask; Bollingen Series 46; Princeton: Princeton University Press, 1971); and idem, *Patterns in Comparative Religion* (trans. Rosemary Sheed; New York: World, 1963), 367–85.

16. Maximilian Streck, *Assurbanipal und die letzten assyrischen Könige bis zum Untergange Ninivehs* (Vorderasiatische Bibliothek 7; Leipzig: J. C. Hinrichs, 1916), 6–7. Compare Alasdair Livingstone, *Court Poetry and Literary Miscellanea* (SAA; Helsinki: Helsinki University Press, 1989), 27 ("Assurbanipal's Coronation Hymn," lines 20–22).

17. שכר is difficult. See *HALOT* and commentaries. I cannot follow E. Dhorme's solution, which artificially contrasts limits imposed by doors and bars to limits set by divine word. See Édouard Dhorme, *Le livre de Job* (Paris: Gabalda, 1926), 528.

18. E.g., Atra-ḫasîs, 15–16; BE 39099 (x) 6–7, reverse ii 18–19, 23, 39–40. Wilfred G. Lambert, A. R. Millard, and Miguel Civil, *Atra-ḫasîs: The Babylonian Story of the Flood, with the Sumerian Flood Story* (Oxford: Oxford University Press, 1969), 42–43, 116–21, 166 note.

This ancient pattern of wise building and filling first appears in Mesopotamian royal inscriptions, which, in spite of generic differences, exhibit a great deal of continuity from their Sumerian beginnings to their later Babylonian and Assyrian manifestations and, however indirectly, their biblical adaptations.[19] While one of the earliest hymnic exemplars of the pattern, Gudea's famous cylinders, is also one of the most elaborate and rich, later Neo-Assyrian kings contemporary with the biblical monarchy could distill the complex process of building into lapidary, proverblike terms that embodied the twofold *process* outlined above. Such summary statements occur in the context of larger *res gestae* inscriptions. One such statement from Esarhaddon declares simply, "That house I built, I completed. With splendor I filled it.[20] Another text gives a variant summary statement, accompanied by a basic declaration of the *purpose* of temple building. After recounting the rich building materials used, Esarhaddon boasts,

> I built and completed it [a temple in Assur]. For life [lit., my life], for length of days, for the stability of my reign, for the welfare of my posterity, for the safety of my priestly throne, for the overthrow of my enemies, *for the success of the harvest(s) of Assyria, for the welfare of Assyria,* I built it.[21]

Here, national life, cosmic fertility, and well-being are all connected to the god's house, built and provisioned by the king, a point reinforced by the *inclusio,* "I built (it)." The temple and its resident god must be provided for—this being the fundamental purpose of human existence—but the temple's well-being also reciprocally ensures that the cosmic realm of Assyria will be richly provisioned. In reciprocal fashion (*do ut des*), the temple god ensures military victory and conquest, which in turn ensures the material provision of temple and royalty. Hence, the frequent sequence of military campaigns followed by building accounts in Assyrian inscriptions. This pattern of victory and building also informs mythic texts such as *Enūma elish* so that the building–filling topos per se can be a generic subunit in a larger mythic-historical pattern, which Israel also adapted.

The ritual culmination of the building–filling topos appears in verbal and graphic representations that move from building to celebratory banquets of abundance.[22]

---

19. A. K. Grayson, "Assyria and Babylonia," *Or* 49 (1980): 142, 148. See also Jacob Klein, "Building and Dedication Hymns in Sumerian Literature," *Acta Sumerologica* 11 (1989): 28, 35–6; Victor A. Hurowitz, *I Have Built You an Exalted House: Temple Building in the Bible in Light of Mesopotamian and Northwest Semitic Writings* (JSOTSup 115; Sheffield: JSOT Press, 1992); Averbeck, "Sumer."

20. Esarhaddon in *ARAB*, 2.700B. For further examples, see Hurowitz, *I Have Built You an Exalted House*, 117, 213, 214, 235–42.

21. My emphasis; *ARAB*, 2.702.

22. See the appendix "Temple Building and Fertility," in Hurowitz, *I Have Built You an Exalted House*, 322–33. The king's palace is also an emblem of fertility, one of the functions of palace gardens. Mirko Novák, "The Artificial Paradise: Programme and Ideology of Royal Gardens," in *Sex and Gender in the Ancient Near East. Part II: Proceedings of the XLVIIe Rencontre Assyriologique Internationale, Helsinki* (ed. Simo Parpola and Robert M. Whiting; Helsinki: University of Helsinki Press, 2002), 443–60.

Examples include the banquet plaque of Urnanshe, the stele of Assurnasirpal II, Lady Wisdom's house building and banquet (Prov 9:1–6), and the dedication feast of Solomon's Temple (1 Kgs 8:1–5).[23] Victor Hurowitz and Jacob Klein call this generic element the "dedication," in which the divine or human resident entered the house with joy and celebratory abundance.[24] Dedication inscriptions may also be devoted to other artifacts, such as boats and chariots.[25]

2. Building and Filling/Provisioning with Wisdom

In ancient Mesopotamian as in biblical thought, humans build houses and make things "with wisdom." This assertion is meant literally in that temples, palaces, and ordinary homes with their furnishings are well built for strength, stability, beauty, majesty, and so forth. But the ancients also used house building, among other metaphors, to express cosmic creation. In the Bible, house building and filling is the fundamental metaphoric domain for divine creation.[26] The thing known (house building) is used to help readers understand something less known, that is, wisdom, creation, and divine activity.

Since linguistic units, including metaphors, have meaning only within their systemic semantic fields,[27] partial images or metaphors of building and filling houses necessarily presuppose the larger metaphoric domain of houses as their implicit meaning-context.[28] That is, reference to a door or a window implies a house, as does lay-

---

23. See Richard J. Clifford, *Proverbs* (OTL; Louisville: Westminster John Knox, 1999), 103, who adduces also *KTU*, 1.4.VI-VII; *ANET*, 134. For Assurnasirpal II, see Donald J. Wiseman, "A New Stela of Aššur-Naṣir-Pal II," *Iraq* 14 (1952): 24–44; pls. 2–6; *ANET*, 588–60 (with further examples); for Urnanshe, see Henri Frankfort, *The Art and Architecture of the Ancient Orient* (Pelican History of Art; New Haven: Yale University Press, 1954), 70–71, no. 73; *ANEP*, no. 427. In this plaque, the top half pictures the king building, the bottom, feasting.

24. Hurowitz, *I Have Built You an Exalted House*, 44, 92, 95, 260–84; Klein, "Building and Dedication Hymns," 27–67.

25. Klein, "Building and Dedication Hymns."

26. "Aber im Gegensatz zu Ägypten sind in der hebräischen Bibel die biologischen Metaphern marginal, die artifizialistischen [i.e., technical] dominieren. . . . Die artifizialistischen Metaphern sind für die hebräische Bibel typisch" (Keel, "Altägyptische und biblische Weltbild," 35). But an inspection of biblical passages shows that not only does creation in the Hebrew Bible involve the technical skills of house building and provisioning (as with furnishings), but also the biological ones of agricultural growth and provision. Keel's parade example, Psalm 104, testifies amply to this.

27. This linguistic fact means that understanding requires knowledge both of an expression's paradigmatic and its syntagmatic relations. For these concepts, see John Lyons, *Introduction to Theoretical Linguistics* (London: Cambridge University Press, 1979), 70–81.

28. For linguistically based metaphor theory, see George Lakoff and Mark Johnson, *Metaphors We Live By* (Chicago: University of Chicago Press, 1980); Andrew Goatly, *The Language of Metaphors* (London: Routledge, 1997); and Pierre van Hecke, "Are People Walking After or Before God: On the Metaphorical Use of הלך אחרי and הלך לפני," OLP 28 (1997): 37–71. On architectural metaphors of creation in wisdom texts, see Leo G. Perdue, *Wisdom and Creation: The Theology of Wisdom Literature* (Nashville: Abingdon, 1994), 82–83, 90–91, 170–72.

ing a foundation or finishing a roof. Such partial metaphors mean that the larger metaphoric domain is implicitly present even when it is not mentioned in a text. Similarly, houses themselves make sense only within the wider material and cognitive worlds in which they exist. A literal house presupposes the natural world around it, along with the products of human culture, such as roads, agriculture, towns, social structures and so forth. In sum, these basic cultural metaphors imply a material-cognitive world.

Kings (human or divine) or their counselors archetypically demonstrate their wisdom by building (big) houses[29] and providing for them. The profound association of (building) great houses and royalty is evident in the semantic history of Semitic and other languages. The metaphor of creation as building has left its traces in the history of the common Semitic root *bny*, "build/create" (see בנה in Gen 2:22). Akkadian has *banû*, "create," and Ugaritic has *bny*, which means "to build" as a verb and "architect, builder, creator" as a noun, while *bnwt* means "creatures," as in the epithet of El, *bny bnwt* "creator/builder of creatures."[30]

To "fill" a house, gods and kings must also make the earth fruitful—mainly by controlling waterworks—so as to fill cosmic and ordinary "buildings" with good things. The assumption of this worldview is so basic and pervasive that it crops up in unexpected places. For example, the demonstration of Hammurabi's "wisdom" in the prologue to his Law Code is far less concerned with justice per se (contrast the epilogue) than with building numerous houses (temples) and with provisioning them, their environs, and the people who depend on them.[31] The execution of justice with wisdom (epilogue xlvii, 9–58) is grounded in a cosmic wisdom that secures a stable and provident world. Thus the curse on those who undo Hammurabi's work: "May the god Ea . . . the sage among the gods, all-knowing (*apkal ilī mudē mimma šumšu*) . . . deprive him of understanding and wisdom, and may he lead him into confusion; may he dam up his rivers at the source (*nārātišu ina nagbim liskir*); may he not allow any life-sustaining grain in his land" (epilogue xlix, 98-l, 13). The curse, "dam up his rivers at the source," is a pun, for *nagbu* is not only the "watery depths," but also the "source" of wisdom where Ea dwells in the Abzu. The pun is apparent from the preceding context and from the contrast with the prologue's description of Hammurabi as the "wise one, the organizer, he who has mastered all wisdom (*šu ikšudu nagab uršim*)" (prologue iv 7–10). Compare also the opening of the Standard Version of Gilgamesh (I, 1), "He who saw (into) the source [of wisdom] (*ša nagba imuru*), into the foundations of the earth/land." Here *nagbu* refers not only to the deep waters which Gilgamesh plumbs but also to the wisdom he achieves through his quest. At the end

---

29. See the important essay, Ronald F. G. Sweet, "The Sage in Akkadian Literature: A Philological Study," in *The Sage in Israel and the Ancient Near East* (ed. John G. Gammie and Leo G. Perdue; Winona Lake, Ind.: Eisenbrauns, 1990), 45–65.

30. For related terms and meanings, see *AHw* I, 103; *CAD* B, 83ff.; G. del Olmo Lete and J. Sanmartín, *Diccionario de la Lengua Ugarítica* (AuOrSup; Barcelona: Editorial AUSA, 1996), 113–14.

31. Texts cited from Martha T. Roth, *Law Collections from Mesopotamia and Asia Minor* (SBLWAW; Atlanta: Scholars Press, 1995), 71–142.

(as at the beginning of the epic), the only monument to Gilgamesh's wisdom will be what he builds: the mighty walls of Uruk, whose foundations were laid by the "seven sages" (I, 9–21; XI, 314–20).[32]

In Mesopotamia, building was a matter of divine command and agency and of human imitation of the divine wisdom in building. A prayer of Esarhaddon says this explicitly:

> O ye creators of gods and goddesses, build the structure with your own hands, the abode of your exalted divinity. Whatever is in your hearts, so let it be done, without any deviations from the command of your lips. The skilled (*lit.*, wise) artificers whom you called to carry out this commission,—like Ea, their creator, grant unto them the high(est) wisdom, so that their strength and skill, at your exalted command, may accomplish, through the craftsmanship of Nin-igi-kug [= Ea], what their hands undertake.[33]

In Assyria, all elements of the wisdom-building-provisioning topos are already present in the Middle Assyrian inscriptions of Tiglath-pileser I (1114–1076 B.C.E.).[34] He writes, "That cedar palace I built with understanding and skill (and) called it Egal-lugalsharrakurkurra, 'Palace of the King of All [Lands].'"[35] Assurnasirpal II (883–859 B.C.E.), in the famous Banquet Stele cited above, declares, "with the cunning (*ina ḫi-sa-at lib-bi-ia*) which the god Ea, king of the Abzu, extensively wise (*uz-nu rapaštu* [*tu*]), gave to me, the city Kalach I took in hand for renovations. . . . I founded therein a palace. . . ."[36] He goes on to talk of his water works (the "Canal of Abundance") and the orchards he planted. In a description of the dedication feast of the palace, which is unique in Assyrian royal inscriptions, he calls it "the palace full of wisdom."[37]

The original home of this composite topos (building and filling/provisioning *with wisdom*) is in Mesopotamian royal inscriptions, whatever the macrogenre or cultural metanarrative that includes it: hymns to temples or cultic objects (Gudea), foundation deposits, *res gestae* in Assyria, or myth (*Enūma elish*) in Assyria or Babylon. Again, an inscription of Esarhaddon, which concerns building Nineveh, begins with a conventional statement of his piety and god-given wisdom:[38]

---

32. Texts cited from Simon Parpola, *The Standard Babylonian Epic of Gilgamesh* (SAACT 1; Helsinki: Neo-Assyrian Text Corpus Project, 1997).

33. *ARAB* 2.670; cf. Psalm 127.

34. A. K. Grayson, *ARI*, 16–17, 18–19, 28–29.

35. Grayson, *ARI*, 29, para. 105 (77).

36. Grayson, *ARI*, 173, para. 677 (20); Wiseman, "A New Stela," 33, lines 22–23.

37. Grayson, *ARI*, 175, para. 682 (102). Irene Winter objects to this translation and prefers to translate as an epithet: "'Palace of all the Wisdom of Kalhu'"; see Irene J. Winter, "'Seat of Kingship'/'a Wonder to Behold': The Palace as Construct in the Ancient Near East," *Ars Orientalis* 23 (1993): 37 n. 85. The text is ekal kul-lat ni-me-qi ša (al)Kal-i, in Wiseman, "A New Stela," 34, line 104. Compare "Ea [abandoned] Eridu, the house of wisdom" (ᵘʳᵘE-ri-du ᵈÉ-a bīt(É) ne-me-qe/i), Epic of Tukulti-Ninurta, col. I, B, obv. 42, in Peter B. Machinist, "The Epic of Tukulti-Ninurta I: A Study in Middle Assyrian Literature" (Ph.D. diss., Yale University, 1978), 64–65.

38. For the conventional or generic character of this language, see E. D. Van Buren, who cites Daniel

the king who from his youth has feared the word of Aššur, Šamaš, Bēl, and Nabû, and who revered their strength. With the great understanding ([*ina*] *karši rit-pa-*[*še*]) and comprehensive skill ([*ḫa-s*]*is-si pal-ke-*[*e*]) which prince Nudimmud, the *apkallu* of the gods, gave me . . . [gap].[39]

Later Esarhaddon carries the work basket himself, while the people work a year with pleasure and joy building Eḫursaggula ("the House of the Great Mountain"). To the amazement of onlookers, he "fills" the house with splendid wealth (*lu-le-e ú-mal-li*),[40] specifically with the rich, odoriferous woods of the Lebanese mountains, as well as gold plating for doors and furnishings. Things in disorder are restored, and the whole "shines like the sun." Then Aššur and his attendant gods take their rightful place and are provided with a great feast. The king is named "house builder" and celebrates with a three-day feast for humans.[41] Like Ahiqar, the builders who work for Esarhaddon are called *ummânū*.[42] In the same manner that the gods make plans, so do the chief builders: "Competent (*le-ʾ-u-ti*) architects, who make plans (*mu-kin-nu giš-ḫur-ri*), I gathered together."[43]

Similarly, Solomon's legendary wisdom is demonstrated by his building of divine and human houses, in providing his kingdom with overflowing wealth, and in his administration of justice. The queen of Sheba is astounded at Solomon's wisdom, especially in the matters of building and provisioning his house (1 Kgs 10:4–8, 23–24; par. 2 Chr 9:3–7). In Ecclesiastes, the wise Qoheleth describes himself in Solomonic fashion as one who builds and provides: "I built for myself houses/I planted for myself vineyards . . ." (Qoh 2:4).[44] So also, the kings and counselors of old in Job's lament are those "who (re)built ruins for themselves . . . who filled their houses with silver (Job 3:14–15). These and many other texts display our ancient pattern of wise building and provisioning by planting and filling houses with good things.[45]

David Luckenbill, *ARAB* 1.528, 804; 2.651, 670, 659 C, D 915. E. D. Van Buren, *The Flowing Vase and the God with Streams* (Berlin: Hans Schoetz, 1933), 9–10.

39. A variant form of the topos appears in Riekele Borger, *Die Inschriften Asarhaddons Königs von Assyrien* (AfOB 9; Osnabrück: Biblio-Verlag, 1967) 18; Bab. A, episode 15.

40. Borger, *Inschriften Asarhaddons*, 4; cf. 22, Bab. 26 E.; 25, Bab. 35 A, C, F;

41. Borger, *Inschriften Asarhaddons*, 5–6.

42. Borger, *Inschriften Asarhaddons*, 19. Despite some recent objections, in the light of Akkadian and Aramaic evidence, it is best to take אמון in Prov 8:30 as cognate with *ummânu*. See Richard J. Clifford, *Proverbs*, ad loc., and Henri Cazelles, "*Aḥiqar, Ummân* and *Amun* and Biblical Wisdom Texts," in *Solving Riddles and Untying Knots: Biblical, Epigraphic, and Semitic Studies in Honor of Jonas C. Greenfield* (ed. Ziony Zevit et al.; Winona Lake, Ind.: Eisenbrauns, 1995), 45–55; Jonas C. Greenfield, "The Seven Pillars of Wisdom (Prov. 9:1)—A Mistranslation," *JQR* 76 (1985): 13–20.

43. Borger, *Inschriften Asarhaddons*, 21; Bab. 24, B and C.

44. Cf. Sargon II, *ARAB* 2.119. Further ancient Near Eastern background in Choon-Leong Seow, "Qohelet's Autobiography," in *Fortunate the Eyes That See: Essays in Honor of David Noel Freedman* (ed. Astrid B. Beck et al.; Grand Rapids: Eerdmans, 1995), 275–87.

45. The description of the ideal king's palace and gardens in Homer's account of King Alcinous of Phaeacia appears to be a Greek reflex of this tradition (*Od.* 7.81–132). See Martin L. West, *The East Face of Helicon: West Asiatic Elements in Greek Poetry and Myth* (Oxford: Clarendon, 1997), 251–52, and *pas-*

In the Hebrew Bible especially, this pattern commonly describes divine creation. In the Priestly creation account (Gen 1:1–2:3), the metaphor of building and filling lies largely beneath the surface.[46] Yet, Hurowitz rightly concludes that

> By employing building terminology in the Creation story, the priestly author has done nothing new, but has joined other biblical writers who describe the world as a building, the Creation as an act of building, and the Creator as a wise, knowledgeable and discerning architect.[47]

In Genesis, the cosmos itself is implicitly God's house or temple/palace.[48] The "rooms" of creation are built (by a process of royal commands and separations) in the first three days. The topos is continued (something not noticed by Hurowitz) in the next three days, when the corresponding realms are *filled*, and both animals and humans receive the explicit blessing, "be fruitful and *fill*" the earth and its realms (1:22, 28). Since, as noted, the motif of filling and provisioning is also part of royal building accounts, the case of Hurowitz and others for the building background to Genesis 1 is strengthened. Thus when *Gen. Rab.* 1.1 brings Prov 8:30 to bear, it is not imposing an alien wisdom on Genesis 1 but making explicit aspects of the text's implicit metaphoric domain.

> In human practice, when a mortal king builds a palace, he builds it not with his own skill [דעת] but with the skill of an architect [root אמן]. The architect moreover does not build it out of his head, but employs plans and diagrams to know how to arrange the chambers and the wicket doors. Thus God consulted [lit., looked into] the Torah and created the world.[49]

As suggested, the wisdom of God in creation is regularly portrayed in architectural and building terms. "To weigh the wind, to mete out the waters by measure, to make a limit for the rain . . ." (Job 28:25). "Who measured the waters by the hand-

---

sim. On *Od.* 7.86–94, see Sarah P. Morris, *Daidalos and the Origins of Greek Art*, 83–87, and 73–141. Morris traces the tradition through Ugarit and, following Mark S. Smith, considers Kothar-wa-Ḥasîs a forerunner of Hephaistos.

46. The "sanctuary symbolism" of J's Eden account makes explicit on the microcosmic level what P leaves implicit on the macrocosmic level. See Gordon J. Wenham, "Sanctuary Symbolism in the Garden of Eden Story," in *Proceedings of the Ninth World Congress of Jewish Studies* Division A (Jerusalem: Magnes, 1985), 19–25.

47. Hurowitz, *I Have Built You an Exalted House*, 242.

48. S. Dean McBride, "Divine Protocol: Genesis 1:1–2:3 as Prologue to the Pentateuch," in *God Who Creates: Essays in Honor of W. Sibley Towner* (ed. William P. Brown and S. Dean McBride; Grand Rapids: Eerdmans, 2000), 11–15; Jon D. Levenson, *Creation and the Persistence of Evil: The Jewish Drama of Divine Omnipotence* (San Francisco: Harper & Row, 1988), 78–99; John M. Lundquist, "What Is a Temple? A Preliminary Typology," in *The Quest for the Kingdom of God: Studies in Honor of George E. Mendenhall* (ed. Herbert B. Huffmon et al.; Winona Lake, Ind.: Eisenbrauns, 1983), 205–19.

49. Harry Freedman, *Midrash Rabbah: Genesis* (London: Soncino, 1951), 1. See also Isidore Epstein, *The Babylonian Talmud: Seder Nezikin* (London: Soncino, 1935), *Sanh.* 38a, 240–41. Such passages as Sir 24:23 assume the equivalence of Torah and Wisdom.

ful [a measure, like our "foot"], and measured the heavens with a span, meted the earth's dust with measure, weighed the mountains with a scale and the hills with a balance?" (Isa 40:12). Such descriptions are almost casual in their assumption that god's wisdom in creation is best presented in architectural terms. The stability of creation and of buildings is frequently expressed by the architectural verb "establish" (כון) and by the negative "it will not topple" (לא/בל ת/ימוט Pss 93:1; 96:10), but so is the stability of an idol made by the wise craftsman (חרש חכם; Isa 40:2). Again, the Lord "set (יסד) the earth on its pillars as a foundation, it shall not totter" (Ps 104:5; cf. v. 24 on God's wisdom in creation). The careful architectural language of Job 38 is widely recognized (38:4–6, 8–11), but the divine speeches also speak of provisioning the cosmos (e.g., 38:25–27, 34–41), another instance of our twofold topos.

In Isa 66:1–2 YHWH declares, "The heavens are my throne, and the earth is my footstool. What sort of house might you build for me? Where might be my resting place?" The individual metaphors "throne" and "footstool" do not stand alone but imply the entire "house," that is, the cosmos itself. This is clearly implied by the merismus "heavens" and "earth," and is made explicit by בית in v. 2. Ironically, "throne" and "footstool" suggest that the cosmos itself is not a big enough house for God (cf. 1 Kgs 8:27). Similarly, the homology of temple and cosmos is implicit in Isa 6:1–8, as shown in the triple parallelism of "filling" the "house" with *robe* and *smoke* and the earth with *glory* (cf. Exod 40:34–35; 1 Kgs 8:11). Psalm 104:24 summarizes the wise acts of making and filling well:[50] "How many are the things You have made, O Lord; You made them all with wisdom (בחכמה), / The earth is full (מלאה) of your creatures" (cf. Prov 1:13; 3:20; 9:2, 5; 24:3; 31:15).

3. Key Biblical "Wisdom" Texts

The above materials provide background to the well-known couplets from Prov 3:19–20, which describe divine creation of the cosmos and its provisioning through water. Surprisingly, the relation of this text to house building remains largely unexplored.[51] Consequently, its significance for understanding biblical wisdom has been inadequately appreciated. Greater clarity here may further the discussion concerning Israelite wisdom and creation.[52] The text reads:

---

50. For discussion of building in Psalm 104, see Keel, "Altägyptische und biblische Weltbilder," 35, 42–43.

51. Independent exceptions to this observation are Gerald T. Sheppard, *The Future of the Bible: Beyond Liberalism and Literalism* (Toronto: United Church Publishing House, 1990), 119–27; Raymond C. Van Leeuwen, "Liminality and Worldview in Proverbs 1–9," *Semeia* 50 (1990): 111–44; idem, "Building God's House: An Exploration in Wisdom," in *The Way of Wisdom: Essays in Honor of Bruce K. Waltke* (ed. J. I. Packer and S. K. Soderlund; Grand Rapids: Zondervan, 2000), 204–11.

52. Roland E. Murphy, "Wisdom and Creation," *JBL* 104 (1985): 3–11; Peter Doll, *Menschenschöpfung und Weltschöpfung in der alttestamentlichen Weisheit* (SBS 117; Stuttgart: Verlag Katholisches Bibelwerk, 1985); Richard J. Clifford and John J. Collins, eds., *Creation in Biblical Traditions* (CBQMS 24; Washington, D.C.: Catholic Biblical Association, 1992); Leo Perdue, *Wisdom*; Richard J. Clifford, *Cre-*

כּוֹנֵן שָׁמַיִם בִּתְבוּנָה   יהוה בְּחָכְמָה יָסַד־אָרֶץ
וּשְׁחָקִים יִרְעֲפוּ־טָל   בְּדַעְתּוֹ תְּהוֹמוֹת נִבְקָעוּ

The LORD *by wisdom founded* the earth, *establishing* the heavens *by skill,*
By his knowledge the deeps were split,[53] and the clouds drop dew.

Within Proverbs, a related, two-couplet saying appears in 24:3–4:

בִּתְבוּנָה יִתְכּוֹנָן   בְּחָכְמָה יִבָּנֶה בָּיִת
כָּל־הוֹן יָקָר וְנָעִים   וּבְדַעַת חֲדָרִים יִמָּלְאוּ

By wisdom a house is built, *by skill* it is *established.*
By knowledge (its) rooms are filled, with all (sorts of) wealth, precious and
lovely.

The striking parallel between these two passages has received surprisingly little
attention, perhaps because of form critical traditions that interpret the generic differences between Proverbs 1–9 and 10–29 as signs of discrete social-historical and ideo-
logical locations.[54] Most notable in this regard is Peter Doll's treatment of Prov

---

ation Accounts in the Ancient Near East and in the Bible (CBQMS 26; Washington, D.C.: Catholic Biblical
Association, 1994), 177–97.

53. בקע refers to the delimiting *separation* of waters and dry land, and the subsequent apportioning
of the waters to their respective places. Compare Ps 74:15; the point is that creation occurs by separations
and apportionment, signally of dry and wet, light and dark (Psalm 104 *passim*; Prov 8:27–29; Job 38:8–
11; Jer 5:22). Contrast Michael V. Fox, *Proverbs 1–9* (AB 18A; New York: Doubleday, 2000), ad loc.

54. Peter Doll uncovers only three "hymnic" parallels to Prov 3:19–20: Pss 104:24; 136:5; Jer 10:12–
16 (*Menschenschöpfung und Weltschöpfung,* 48–51). However, as Clifford notes, Prov 3:12–26 "is not a
hymn" (Clifford, *Creation Accounts,* 181 n. 8; see further pp. 178–85 and 151–62 for Clifford's critique of
Rainer Albertz, *Weltschöpfung und Menschenschöpfung: Untersucht bei Deutero-jesaja, Hiob und in den
Psalmen* [Calwer Theologische Monographien 3; Stuttgart: Calwer, 1974]). Otto Plöger (*Sprüche Salomos
(Proverbia)* [BKAT 17; Neukirchen-Vluyn: Neukirchener Verlag, 1984], 37–38, 279) connects 24:2–3 to
3:19 (not 3:20!) and 9:1; 14:1, but not to Exodus or 1 Kings. He sees the relation of "wisdom" and "skill"
to Prov 8:1 but fails to see that "wisdom/skill/knowledge" is a stereotypical pattern. Michael V. Fox (*Proverbs
1–9* [AB 18A; New York: Doubleday, 2000], 160) connects 3:19–20 with 24:3–4, but does not note the
tripartite wisdom formula for building. He does observe the parallel pattern of "creation" and "provision."
Clifford (*Proverbs* [OTL; Louisville: Westminster John Knox Press, 1999], 55) notes the parallels in Jer
10:12 (= 51:15; see 32:17; Ps 65:7): "He made the earth by his might, established the world by his wisdom,/
and by his understanding he stretched out the heavens." But he does not connect 3:19–20 or 24:2–3 with
Exodus or 1 Kings. R. Norman Whybray (*Proverbs* [NCBC; Grand Rapids: Eerdmans, 1994], 343-44)
suggests literary dependence of 24:3–4 on 3:19–20 and sees the connection with 9:1 and 14:1 but makes
no connection to Exodus and 1 Kings. Crawford H. Toy (*Proverbs* [ICC; New York: Scribner's, 1902], 70-
72, 442) does not connect Prov 3:19–20 to 24:2–3, or Proverbs to Exodus or 1 Kings. Roland E. Murphy
(*Proverbs* [WBC 22; Nashville: Thomas Nelson, 1998]) relates the two passages in Proverbs (and Jer 10:12),
saying that "the Lord . . . imitates human building (cf. 24:3)" (p. 22). He seems more correct when he says
later, "Just as the Lord 'founded' the earth by wisdom (Prov 3:19), so humans need the same for building
their 'house'" (p. 180). J. van der Ploeg (*Spreuken* [Roermond en Maaseik: J. J. Romen, 1952], 83) connects 24:3–4 only to 9:1. Franz Delitzsch (*Salomonisches Spruchbuch* [Leipzig: Dörffling u. Franke, 1873;
repr., Giessen: Brunnen Verlag, 1985], 380–81) connects 24:3–4 to 3:19 only with reference to the parallel of בנה and כון. André Barucq (*Le livre des Proverbes* [SB; Paris: Gabalda, 1964], 85) connects 24:3–4 to

3:19–20, which presupposes a separation of texts in Proverbs 1–9 from those in 10–29 on form-critical grounds.[55] Following Claus Westermann, he believes that the "tradition" of world creation stems from "the hymn" and is separate from the tradition of creating humans found in Proverbs 10–29.[56] In spite of his implicit claim to completeness (55), Doll ignores even the tight connection between Prov 3:19–20 and 24:3–4, as well as the further parallels with Exodus and 1 Kings adduced below. But fundamental worldview concepts are not bound to a genre. A saying can give utterance to the same concept as a hymn, a didactic speech, a narrative, or a royal building report. And one utterance may rest implicitly on a presupposition expressed conceptually only in another genre. Doll also assumes that world creation is a development in a hypothetical third, theological stage of Israel's wisdom (78). But this hypothesis is rooted in a modern disjunction of sacred and secular that misconstrues the unitary nature of ancient Near Eastern worldviews—including Israel's.

Though sections of Proverbs may stem from discrete sociohistorical locations,[57] ancient cultures nonetheless manifest common understandings that endure for centuries and include diverse social groups. Proverbs 3:19–20 occurs as a subgeneric element in a long blessing, or macarism (3:13–20/26),[58] set among the instructions and wisdom poems of Proverbs 1–9. This blessing is closely related to the poems about Lady Wisdom and those spoken by Wisdom or Folly (1:20–33; 8:1–36; 9:1–6, 13–18). It functions—as does the creation section of Proverbs 8 (i.e., 8:22–31)—as a divine, cosmic warrant for the claims of blessing made in the macarism and in Wisdom's speech, respectively.[59] In Proverbs 10–29, however, shorter sayings and admonitions predominate—generic units that assume a relative independence and whose literary context functions mostly on an implicit level by way of juxtaposition or distant parallels.[60] Yet language and conceptuality do cross generic boundaries, within and

---

9:9–19 [?]; 8:21; 14:1. Helmut Ringgren (*Sprüche, Prediger, Das Hohe Lied, Klagelieder, Das Buch Esther* [ATD 16; Göttingen: Vandenhoeck & Ruprecht, 1981], 23, 96) states no connections at all. Berend Gemser (*Sprücche Salomos* [HAT 16; Tübingen: Mohr-Siebeck, 1963], 30) strongly connects 3:19–20 to 14:1; 24:3.

55. Peter Doll, *Menschenschöpfung und Weltschöpfung*, 48–51.

56. "[B]ei der Überlieferung des Motives vom Dabeisein der Weisheit bei der Weltschöpfung handelt es sich um einen Überlieferungszweig der Weltschöpfungstradition des Hymnus" (Doll, *Menschenschöpfung und Weltschöpfung*, 78). See also Albertz, *Weltschöpfung und Menschenschöpfung*, esp. 54–89. In keeping with his focus on "hymnic" material in Second Isaiah, Job, and the Psalms, Albertz's ancient Near Eastern and "primitive cultural" comparative material is all taken from the prayer (*Gebet*) genre. The assumption of hymnic genre has dictated his selection of comparative material.

57. R. Norman Whybray, *The Composition of Proverbs* (JSOTSup 99; Sheffield: JSOT, 1994). Contrast Michael V. Fox, "The Social Location of the Book of Proverbs," in *Texts, Temples, and Traditions: A Tribute to Menahem Haran* (ed. Michael V. Fox et al; Winona Lake, Ind.: Eisenbrauns, 1996), 227–39.

58. Fox, *Proverbs 1–9*, 156; Clifford, *Creation Accounts*, 179–81, 184.

59. Clifford, *Creation Accounts*, 178–79, 184. The parallel three-part structure of both poems was noted earlier by Gerhard von Rad, *Weisheit in Israel* (Neukirchen-Vluyn: Neukirchener Verlag, 1970), 197 n 4; Eng. trans., *Wisdom of Israel* (Nashville: Abingdon, 1972), 151, n. 4.

60. For the importance of distant parallelism in Proverbs, see Dennis Pardee, *Ugaritic and Hebrew Poetic Parallelism: A Trial Cut ('nt I and Proverbs 2)* (VTSup; Leiden: Brill, 1988); and Daniel C. Snell, *Twice-Told Proverbs and the Composition of the Book of Proverbs* (Winona Lake, Ind.: Eisenbrauns, 1993).

without Proverbs.[61] More to the point, however, Prov 3:19–20 and 24:3–4 are both adaptations and combinations of the topical elements, noted above, in royal-building inscriptions. That is, they combine the general building–filling/providing topos (which may be expanded or contracted according to generic need) with a statement concerning the wisdom of the builder or the enterprise. Thus, each unit (3:19–20; 24:3–4) presents *in nuce* an Israelite formulation of ancient Near Eastern ideas of building and filling with wisdom.

First, houses are built and "established/made solid" (כון) by wisdom. This idea is not peripheral to Israel's notion of wisdom but foundational, as its frequency within Proverbs shows (9:1; 14:1; 24:3; cf. 12:7; 14:11; 15:25; 21:12 [?]; 24:27). Even animals are included in this pattern of wise or foolish house building (30:24–26) and provisioning (6:6–11).

The second motif common to Prov 3:19–20 and 24:3–4 is provisioning or filling the house. The frequency of this basic motif strengthens the conceptual coherence among the subsections of Proverbs at a fundamental level (9:1–6, 13–18; and 3:33; 6:31; 11:29; 15:6, 27; 17:1, 13; 19:14; 24:4; 27:27; 31:11, 15, 21, 27). The "contents" that fill a house can be good or bad, inasmuch as they are acquired by means fair or foul, by wisdom or folly, and inasmuch as they are appropriate or fitting. A striking instance of this ethical polarity in provisioning appears in the use of identical language in Prov 24:4 and in the first parental "lecture" in Prov 1:13. There the wicked robbers say, "We will find *all (sorts of) wealth, precious and lovely*; we will *fill* our *house* with booty" (cf. Ps 112:3; Song 8:7; Sir 1:17; 23:11). The significance of the house imagery in Proverbs only increases when its interaction with the metaphors of "women" and "ways," especially in Proverbs 1–9, is kept in mind (see 2:16–19; 5:2–8; 7:6–27; 8:32–34; 9:1–6, 13–18).[62]

On the cosmic level, the monotheistic provision for creation in Prov 3:20 ("By his knowledge the deeps were split, and the clouds drop dew") finds a polytheistic parallel in a Assyrian cliché that spells out the point of Prov 3:20. After his installation on the throne, Assurbanipal states,

> Adad sent his rains, Ea opened his fountains, the grain grew . . . heavy crops and plenteous yields made the field(s) continuously luxuriant, the orchards yielded a rich harvest, the cattle successfully brought forth their young,—in my reign there was fullness to overflowing, in my years there was plenteous abundance.[63]

When Prov 24:3–4 is set alongside 3:19–20, the significance of the former grows. Both use the same three prepositional phrases in the same order, and likewise employ

---

61. *Pace* Carol A. Newsom, *The Book of Job: A Contest of Moral Imaginations* (New York: Oxford University Press, 2003), who argues that different genres are expressions of distinct "moral imaginations," the latter functioning much as a "wordview" or "cognitive environment." See Alan Dundes, "Folklore Ideas as Units of Worldview," *Journal of American Folklore* 84 (1971): 93–103.

62. Van Leeuwen, "Liminality"; and idem, "The Book of Proverbs," *New Interpreter's Bible* 5 (ed. L. Keck; Nashville: Abingdon, 1997), ad loc.

63. *ARAB* 2.769; cf. 843, 935, 970.

the root כון in the second half line. In terms of *metaphor formation*, we may say that
the description of YHWH's building of the cosmic house is modeled on the building
of human houses or temples by wisdom, skill, and knowledge. But *conceptually*, as
Mircea Eliade and others have shown, in ancient societies such metaphoric representations of reality claim to say something about reality itself:[64] that the norms and mod-
els for human existence and action are found in the primordial cosmic and cultural
events that founded the world and society.[65] This is widely recognized in studies of the
ancient Near East. It is less widely acknowledged to be true of Israel as well. Nonetheless, for Israel the goodness of the primeval creation (and its gradual renewal in the
nation's founding events of exodus, Sinai, and conquest) is the norm for Israel's action
in history and the goal of its history.[66] Though the language of human house building is used metaphorically to portray divine creation, the conceptual message runs
implicitly in the other direction. The divine building of the cosmic house by wisdom
is the model for human house building; human culture is a form of the *imitatio dei*,
especially with reference to God's creation of the cosmos as the house in which all
houses are contained.[67]

   While post-Enlightenment persons may think such ancient ideas absurd—as pro-
jection of realities created or imposed on nature by humans—their truth claim (Hans-
Georg Gadamer) should not be too hastily or presumptuously dismissed.[68] Such ideas
embody the deep insight that human agency or house building must take place in
terms of standards, as it were, built into reality.[69] A bridge that does not take into
account physical laws eventually collapses. So does an empire that ignores justice and
righteousness (see Dan 4:27). Even cruel despots pay lip service to the claims of justice and righteousness—especially when they abuse such claims: "Hypocrisy is the

---

64. See Janet M. Soskice, *Metaphor and Religious Language* (Oxford: Clarendon Press, 1985); and
Dale Launderville, *Piety and Politics: The Dynamics of Royal Authority in Homeric Greece, Biblical Israel, and
Old Babylonian Mesopotamia* (Grand Rapids: Eerdmans, 2003), 25–30.

65. Mircea Eliade, *The Sacred and the Profane: The Nature of Religion* (trans. Willard R. Trask; New
York: Harper & Row, 1961), 20–65.

66. R. Knierim, "Cosmos and History in Israel's Theology," *HBT* 3 (1981): 59–123; repr. in Rolf P.
Knierim, "Cosmos and History," *The Task of Old Testament Theology: Substance, Method and Cases* (Grand
Rapids: Eerdmans, 1995), 171–224. That we are dealing with "re-creation" of the cosmos is evident from
the splitting of the Yam Sup and of the Jordan River. In Eliade's terms, these are repetitions of the primal
separation of the waters at creation. It is this cosmic act of re-creation that causes Rahab to declare that
YHWH alone is "god in heaven above and on earth below" (Josh 2:10–11). See also Jon D. Levenson,
Sinai and Zion: An Entry into the Jewish Bible (Minneapolis: Winston, 1985).

67. Alluding to chaos theory, Schloen speaks of a "'fractal' or recursive hierarchy of households within
households" generated "not through the imposition of an overall structure from above, but through ongo-
ing operation of a simple set of local rules for social interactions." Schloen, *House of the Father*, 59; cf. 91.

68. "Wahrheitsanspruch." Hans-G. Gadamer, *Wahrheit und Methode: Grundzüge einer philosophi-
schen Hermeneutik* (Tübingen: Mohr Siebeck, 1975 [1960]), 21, 31. The notion of art's truth is central to
Gadamer's hermeneutics of understanding (77–96).

69. The best treatment of this aspect of biblical wisdom remains von Rad, *Weisheit in Israel*. Unfortunately, the English translation is often unreliable on basic points.

homage that vice pays to virtue."[70] That human representation of reality is metaphorical does not negate insights into god and cosmos that such representations may communicate.

This imitation of deity—implicit in many biblical texts—appears explicitly in Mesopotamian foundation deposits and inscriptions concerning the building of monumental works: cities, temples, palaces and their accoutrements, irrespective of their cultic or noncultic function.[71] Things are built with the wisdom that the deity gave the builder and, thus, with an insight into the structures and norms of the cosmos pertaining to their building activities—norms that the Sumerians called ME or GIŠ.ḤUR. For instance, it is perhaps Assurbanipal as crown prince who sees his late father, Esarhaddon, in the text called a "Vision of the underworld."[72] In it, Esarhaddon's comprehensive knowledge of and wisdom concerning reality are described in the statement that he is "one who knows (many) things, of broad comprehension, with wide and discerning understanding, *one who studies the design of what holds the earth together.*"[73]

Because of their comparative insignificance, private homes did not usually have inscriptions or foundation deposits. Richard Ellis cites a striking exception, which again affords a parallel to the presuppositions underlying the vocabulary of Prov 24:3–4. The human builder builds with wisdom given by the "builder" of the cosmos:

> I ceremoniously had occupied the house which I had dedicated in the shadow of the temple of Marduk, inside which I dug a well of cold water and which I made large with the august wisdom (*ina ne-me-qí ṣīri*) of Marduk, my lord. I constructed very solidly, with great skill (*ina ḫi-ès-[sa]-at ne-me-qí ma-di-à*), the baked-brick rooms beneath it, which no one knows of. I built completely the whole house, its *gipārus* and its living rooms. . . . May Marduk, my lord, look upon that house and grant it to me as a resting place; may it be reserved for my sons and my grandsons, for my offspring and my descendants forever.[74]

Here Marduk, the Babylonian creator god, takes the place of his divine father, Enki/Ea, as the bestower of wisdom. The well connects the house to the *apsû*, the primordial fount of life-giving waters and wisdom.[75] The builder prays that his house may

---

70. Cf. Charles Malik, "History-Making, History-Writing, History-Interpreting," *Center Journal* 1 (1982): 11–42.

71. Richard S. Ellis, *Foundation Deposits in Ancient Mesopotamia* (New Haven: Yale University Press, 1968), 163–65.

72. Livingstone, *Court Poetry*, xxviii.

73. Cited from Sweet, "Sage," 55. Sweet's essay provides many instances of wisdom and building. Complete text and translation in Livingstone, *Court Poetry*, 75–76, *mu-de-e a-ma-ti ra-pa-áš uz-ni pal-ku-u ka-ra-áš ta-šim-ti ša* GIŠ.ḤUR.MEŠ [= *uṣurāti šá mar-k[as] qaq-qa-ri ḫi-i[tu]*].

74. Ellis, *Foundation*, 174.

75. In temples without wells, a water basin takes this role: "In temples a water-basin, as an image of the *apsû*, was set up in honour of Ea, and he had shrines in many temples. . . ." Van Buren, *Flowing Vase*, 10. While the Solomonic temple demythologizes the waters, the cosmic symbolism of the great "sea" remains evident.

be filled with offspring for generations to come. In early Judaism, Wis 9:8–12 also explicitly draws the connection between God as cosmos builder and Solomon as house builder, with Wisdom as the mediator of architectural wisdom (cf. 7:22; 8:4–6; Prov 8:30). This is the basis of Solomon's universal claim to all types of wisdom, as described in the text. It rivals the Mesopotamian royal claims to universal competence from Shulgi to Esarhaddon.[76] According to Berossus's famous account of the primal *apkallu*, Oannes, the wisdom transmitted to humans is cultural wisdom in the broadest sense,[77] a theme we see also in Aeschylus's version of the Prometheus myth.[78] It was not just that Prometheus brought the gift of fire to mortals but that fire was the *didaskalos technēs pasēs*, the "teacher of every craft" (lines 110–11; cf. 254). Later, Prometheus directly claims that he brought all cultural arts to humans (lines 443–506): "All the arts (*pasai technai*) of mortals come from Prometheus" (line 506). In such narratives, an *apkallu* or Titan mediates divine wisdom. In Proverbs, it is Lady Wisdom.

Thus, in Proverbs, divine creation and provision are the implicit model for the wisdom by which ordinary builders make and "fill" houses. Lady Wisdom herself, whose role in creation is explored below, is represented by the broken word pair, חכמה . . . תבונה, "wisdom . . . skill," not just by "wisdom"[79]—a crucial but sometimes neglected point (Prov 8:1; cf. 2:2; 3:13; 9:1).[80] The word pair reminds one of the double wisdom name of the Ugaritic builder-craftsman god, Kothar-wa-Ḥasis, who was famous for building Baal's palace. The practical connotations of תבונה have been long recognized, but those of חכמה are often denigrated in comparison with presumably more "intellectual" or moral-religious usages. Nonetheless, Lady Wisdom's skill in house building has its human reflex in wise women who "build houses" literally and metaphorically (14:1, based on 9:1; see Ruth 4:11 and 3:11 with Prov 31:10).[81] This formulaic word pair, "wisdom . . . skill" underlies the tripartite formula in Prov 3:19–

---

76. See the "Praise Poems of Šulgi" (Šulgi A and B), available online in transliteration and translation from the Oxford based "The Electronic Text Corpus of Sumerian Literature," http://www-etcsl.orient.ox.ac.uk.

77. See Clifford, *Proverbs*, 24–27; and Claus Wilcke, "Göttliche und menschliche Weisheit im Alten Orient: Magie und Wissenschaft, Mythos und Geschichte," in *Weisheit* (ed. A. Assmann; Munich: Fink, 1991), 259–70. For Berossus, see Stanley M. Burstein, *The Babyloniaca of Berossus* (Sources from the Ancient Near East 1/5; Malibu, Calif.: Undena, 1978).

78. Aeschylus, *Prometheus Bound*, LCL.

79. Compare the hendiadys name of Kothar wa-Hasis ("Skillful and Cunning"), the Canaanite craftsman god famous as the builder of Baal's house. Compare Akkadian *ḥasīsu*, "wisdom." He is identified with Mesopotamian Ea/Aya. See Dennis Pardee in *DDD*, 490–91, s.v., "Koshar"; Mark S. Smith, "Kothar Wa-Hasis, the Ugaritic Craftsman God" (Ph.D. diss.; Yale University, 1985) [University Microfilms International 8600992].

80. In Ezek 28:4–5 the word pair refers to mercantile prowess. By itself, the term תבונה bears connotations of practical competence in areas as diverse as speech (Ps 49:4; Prov 17:27), warfare (Prov 21:30), metallurgy (Hos 13:2), powers of psychological penetration (20:5), and political governance (28:16; cf. Ps 78:72, which reflects a prior literal usage referring to the skilled hands of a shepherd ובתבונות כפיו. Psalm 136:5 describes creation by תבונה alone (cf. Ps 147:5). חכמה and תבונה are comprehensive, global terms which can refer to any area of life (see Eccl 1:13). See further Fox, "Words for Wisdom."

81. See Van Leeuwen, "Proverbs," 138.

20, just as "heaven and earth" has its tripartite expansion in "heaven and earth and sea" (Exod 20:11).[82] The primacy of the word pair over the triplet is evident from the variant construction in Exod 36:1, where דעת is a subsidiary grammatical element after חכמה ... ותבונה, that is, דעת is there a semantic but not a grammatical parallel. Thus, when in Prov 3:13 the blessed person "finds wisdom" and "gets skill," it should be clear that humans pursue a wisdom congruent with that used by God to build the world (3:19). A hymnic fragment in Jeremiah combines this word pair with "strength": "Who made the earth by his strength (בכחו), established (מכין) the world by his wisdom (בחכמתו), and by his skill (בתבונתו) stretched out the heavens" (Jer 10:12 = 51:15). Thus God gives the builder-king Solomon "wisdom" and "skill" (חכמה and תבונה, 1 Kgs 5:9), referring both to his intellectual wisdom (1 Kgs 5:10–14) and to his building activities (1 Kgs 5:15–7:51). Ideally, the king has wisdom as comprehensive as Lady Wisdom's (cf. Wis 7:16–22; 9:8–12). As noted above, this partial account of Solomon's wisdom corresponds to Esarhaddon's and Shulgi's famous boasts to have universal learning and the wisdom of the ancients. But the monuments to these kings' wisdom are their buildings and provision.

Cosmic creation is also the model for building the tabernacle (Exodus) and temple (1 Kings), as has frequently been argued.[83] The sanctuary is a microcosmic house mirroring the macrocosmic house of creation.[84] (Not incidentally, both cosmos and temple are said to be "filled" with the divine "glory"; see Isa 6:3). This imitation of God in building is made explicit by the parallel in Chronicles to 1 Kgs 7:13–14. Hiram blesses God "who made heaven and earth, who has given King David a wise son, 'knowing' skill and insight (יודע שכל ובינה) that he may build a house for the Lord, and a royal palace for himself" (2 Chr 2:11)." What is little noticed, however, is that the prose texts of Exodus and 1 Kings use the same vocabulary, in the same order as Prov 3:19–20 and 24:3–4, to describe the wisdom repertoire of the divine or human builder.[85] God's spirit equips Bezalel to work with the same threefold wisdom that Proverbs claims the Lord used in creation:

אמלא אתו רוח אלהים בחכמה בתבונה ובדעת בכל־מלאכה

---

82. See now Annette Krüger, "Himmel-Erde—Unterwelt: kosmologische Entwürfe in der poetischen Literatur Israels," *Das biblische Weltbild und seine altorientalischen Kontexte* (ed. Bernd Janowski and Beate Ego; FAT 32; Tübingen: Mohr Siebeck, 2001), 65–83.

83. For literature and discussion see Cornelis Houtman, *Exodus* (Historical Commentary on the Old Testament; Leuven: Peeters, 2000), 3.306–8; and McBride, "Divine Protocol," 11–15.

84. This view is found already in Philo (*Mos.* 2.6 [88] and 12 [117ff.]) and Josephus (*Ant.* 3.123, 180–87). One does not have to follow the fanciful allegory in accepting the basic correctness of this position on both exegetical and history-of-religion grounds. For an overview, see Levenson, *Creation and the Persistence of Evil*, 78–99; Elizabeth Bloch-Smith, "'Who Is the King of Glory?' Solomon's Temple and its Symbolism," in *Scripture and Other Artifacts: Essays on the Bible and Archaeology in Honor of Philip J. King* (ed. Michael Coogan et al.; Louisville: Westminster John Knox, 1994), 18–31.

85. Often temples are built with dual or triple agency: the god, the king, and the wise workers; see Psalm 127.

I will fill him with God's spirit, *with wisdom, with skill, and with knowledge* in all (sorts of) workmanship. (Exod 31:3; par. 35:31; variant 36:1; cf. 35:35)[86]

This parallel to the wisdom literature is one of many that link the tabernacle pericopes in Exodus to Proverbs. The tabernacle workers are חכם לב "wise hearted" (Exod 28:3; 31:6; 36:1, 8; of women 35:25; cf. Prov 10:8; 11:29; 16:21; 23:15; variants Job 9:4; 37:24; cf. Prov 2:6). In Exod 35:25–26, "all the wise-hearted women" (כל־אשה חכמת־לב), who weave cloth for the tabernacle "with wisdom" (בחכמה), have their counterpart in the "valiant woman" of Proverbs 31. She manufactures for her "house" the same types of fine cloth found in God's house (Prov 31:13, 19, 21–22, 24–25). The very walls, that is, the structure of the tabernacle itself, are built of cloth woven by women. In the ancient Near East, textile work is archetypically a form of women's wisdom: When Enki, the god of wisdom, introduces weaving and places the goddess Uttu in charge of clothing, it is said that he "perfected the woman's art."[87]

The building accounts of the temple and palace in 1 Kings appear related to P's Exodus account, especially as Kings makes explicit reference to the exodus. For our purposes, the issue of literary influence is not so important, because the topos that both passages employ dictates common patterns of verbal expression. Both passages employ the common pattern of thought that concerns us, a pattern that comes to transcend genre and social locations. The verbal formulation in 1 Kings 7:13 is "virtually identical" with that of Exodus[88] and Proverbs.

וימלא את־החכמה ואת־התבונה ואת־הדעת לעשות כל־מלאכה בנחשת

(God) filled (Hiram) *with wisdom, with skill, and with knowledge* to do all (sorts of) workmanship in bronze. (1 Kgs 7:14)

---

86. The trio of חכמה, תבונה, דעת disappears in the account in 2 Chr 2:11–12, where the king of Tyre calls Solomon a בן חכם יודע שכל ובינה אשר יבנה־בית ליהוה ובית למלכותו, "a wise son [cf. Prov 10:1], knowing expertise and skill, who will build a house for YHWH and a house for his kingship." The trio (with preposition ב) does appear in 11Q5 (= 11QPsᵃ) 6:11–14, but not in the biblical formulaic order; cf. 4Q372 (= 4QapocrJosephᵇ), frag. 2.5, . . . הנ[ותן לו שכל להבין לבנות . . .] "Who gives him expertise to understand building. . . ." Nonetheless, 2 Chronicles 2 maintains the general emphasis on wisdom in building. The builder Hiram/Huram is simply איש חכם, יודע בינה, "a wise man, knowing expertise" (2:12), and the workers are simply החכמים, "the wise ones" (2:6, 13). In this regard, Hebrew חכם displays the same sort of semantic range as does Akkadian *ummânu* and its Aramaic and Hebrew loan words (cf. אמון in Prov 8:30) and the discussion of Clifford, *Proverbs*, 24–27.

87. Kramer and Maier, *Myths of Enki*, 53. Compare the classic relief of a noble woman from Susa and the Egyptian female textile workers in *ANEP*, 42–43, nos. 142–44, and the Neo-Hittite, Iron Age funeral stele from Marash in Carole R. Fontaine, *Smooth Words: Women, Proverbs and Performance in Biblical Wisdom* (JSOTSup 356; London: Sheffield, 2002), 20–22. In Greece, the classic model is Penelope whose standard epithet is "wise" (*periphrōn*, Homer, *Od.* 1.329 and *passim*) weaving and unweaving the robe (*Od.* 1.104–10; 19.148–56). "Athene has endowed her above other women with knowledge of fair handiwork and an understanding heart, and wiles . . . not one [of the famed women of old] was like Penelope in shrewd device . . ." (*Od.* 2.116–22; LCL). The "wisdom" of cunning and of craft is of one cloth here (cf. *Od.* 7.109–11).

88. Noth, *Könige*, 148.

This strong verbal link among Exodus, Kings, and Proverbs has been little noticed by commentators (indeed, even the links within Proverbs are little explored).[89] Strikingly, in spite of the common "architectural" contexts, English translations tend to render the same three Hebrew words (חכמה, תבונה, דעת) differently in Proverbs from what they do in Exodus and Kings, as if something quite different were being discussed! Again, there seems to be no reason for this except that biblical scholars have learned to think of the wisdom literature as something apart, different not only in regard to genre, but different also in social location and conceptuality from the "historical" traditions of Israel. R. N. Whybray's well-known *The Intellectual Tradition in the Old Testament* has exerted considerable influence in this regard.[90] In keeping with Western separation of theoretical and practical reason, Whybray defined wisdom in terms of the "intellectual tradition" found most characteristically in Proverbs, Job, and Ecclesiastes. Conversely, he devalued all instances of the root חכם, referring to "manual skill" as "nonsignificant."[91] Hilaire Duesberg and I. Fransen are a bit more nuanced on חכמה, but they also denigrate the "skill" side of wisdom:

> A son degré le moins élevé, la *hokmah* [*sic*] n'est qu'une habileté d'ordre purement technique, celle de l'artisan expert en son métier manuel, comme le fondeur, le brodeur, le pilote. Les marins de Tyr [Ezek 27:8], les constructeurs du Tabernacle [Exod 31:2–3], Béseléel, Ooliab, Hiram [1 Kgs 7:13–14], ou bien de vulgaires fabricants d'idoles [Isa 40:20] et des pleureuses gagées fortes en voix [Jer 9:16–17; Eng. 9:17–18], tout ce monde est *hakam.*[92]

Yet one must ask, how is it possible that all these diverse activities are understood as *hokmah*? Is there a semantic and conceptual common denominator, or perhaps a diachronic semantic development that enables us to see coherence in the diversity? The question becomes especially acute because P and 1 Kings are clearly concerned with the same archetypical and architectural "wisdom" that appears in Prov 3:19–20; 8:22–31; 9:1; 14:1; and 24:2–3. Because YHWH created the world with such wisdom, it is clear that, as far as Israel was concerned, such wisdom was *not* "moin élevé," nor something "d'ordre purement technique." Rather it is Wisdom per se, from which all other forms of wisdom are derived, as should have been plain from Proverbs 8 and later texts such as Sirach 24 (cf. 1:14, 17; 16:19) and Wisdom 7–9. These great texts show

---

89. Cornelis Houtman does note the connection of Exod 31:3 etc. with Prov 3:19–20, but does not elaborate (*Exodus*, 3.362). See also his treatment and bibliography of the ancient Near Eastern background to the tabernacle building (306–408, 323–25).

90. R. Norman Whybray, *The Intellectual Tradition in the Old Testament* (BZAW 135; Berlin: de Gruyter, 1974).

91. "Such non-significant passages include the 16 occurrences in Exodus where *hokmāh* is the manual skill of those engaged in making priestly garments, the Tabernacle, the Ark etc. . . . They also include I Reg 7₁₄, referring to the craftsman Hiram, and the 6 similar references in Chronicles." Whybray, *Intellectual Tradition*, 83. It is amazing that Whybray did not note the parallels in Prov 3:19–20; 24:3–4!

92. Hilaire Duesberg and I. Fransen, *Les scribes inspirés: Introduction aux livres sapientiaux de la Bible* (Maredsous: Éditions de Maredsous, 1966), 180.

that cosmic house building and related domains such as agriculture are the matrix for nature and human culture alike.[93] Human culture and society, history itself, depend on wise dealing with the cosmos (including human "nature") as given. As God with Wisdom "etches out" (root חקק) the shape of the world (8:27, 29), so human rulers "etch out" (root חקק) the shape of a righteous society (8:15–16).

Craftsmanship or skill *in any area of human endeavor* lies at the heart of biblical wisdom, because wisdom is a concept as wide and all encompassing as creation, which in ancient thought included culture. Thus Whybray's attempt to label the wisdom of "manual skill" as "nonsignificant" seems to read into biblical texts long-standing Western dichotomies of culture and nature (*nomos* and *physis*) and theory and praxis that run counter to the evidence. What is more, attempts to elevate "intellectual" or "spiritual" activities over "practical," material ones impose an alien worldview on biblical wisdom. Biblical metaphors of building and wisdom portray reality and action more integrally—grounded in a creation suffused with the wisdom of God.[94] Polytheistic societies, *mutatis mutandis*, thought similarly about their world and wisdom.

4. A GENERIC ELEMENT: STATEMENT OF [THE BUILDER'S] WISDOM

A further exploration of a generic element in our key biblical texts (Prov 3:19–20; 24:3–4; Exod 31:1–3; 1 Kgs 7:13–14) can help us in our quest to understand wisdom in relation to creation and human affairs. It is the "statement of (the builder's) wisdom." Its origin is in Mesopotamian hymns and annals that celebrate royal building projects. To these may be compared the temple-building account in 1 Kings, as notably done by Hurowitz. Form critically, the temple-building account is by some scholars designated a "report," following M. Noth's "Bericht."[95] Simon De Vries calls it an "Extract from the Book of Solomon's Acts."[96] Burke Long more precisely terms the larger genre "Solomon's Building Activities" with three subunits: "Report of Temple Construction" (6:1–38), "Report of Palace Construction" (7:1–12), and "Report of Temple Furnishings" (7:13–50). But he does not note that the subunit describing Hiram as wise (7:13–14) is a stock, generic element in royal inscriptions that recount the king's *res gestae*. He merely labels it, "introductory setting."[97] In his careful study, Hurowitz simply refers to 1 Kgs 7:13–14 as a "note describing Hiram, the Tyrian artisan," but does not consider its generic function.[98] Richard Averbeck, however, in his

---

93. Note the architectural vocabulary of creation (כון, מוסד, דלתת, מזוזת, פתח) in Proverbs 8 and its relation to 9:1–6. On Wisdom as a bringer of culture, on the pattern of the ancient Near Eastern *apkallu*, see especially Clifford, *Proverbs*, 23–28, 96–101. Contrast Fox, *Proverbs 1–9*, 279–89, 331–45.

94. On this point, in relation to Prov 31:10–31, see Albert Wolters, "Nature and Grace in the Interpretation of Proverbs 31:10–31," *CTJ* 19 (1984) 153–66; also in A. Wolters, *The Song of the Valiant Woman: Studies in the Interpretation of Proverbs 31:10–31* (Carlisle: Paternoster, 2001).

95. Noth, *Könige*, 146–48.

96. Simon J. De Vries, *1 Kings* (WBC; Waco: Word, 1985), 108–9.

97. Burke O. Long, *1 Kings, with an Introduction to Historical Literature* (FOTL; Grand Rapids: Eerdmans, 1984), 90, 92–93.

holistic comparison of the Gudea cylinders with biblical temple-building accounts, does note that "Royal wisdom in association with temple building" is one of the basic "temple-building parallels" between Sumer and the Bible.[99]

Much later and contemporary with the Hebrew monarchy are Neo-Assyrian accounts such as Sennacherib's inscriptions concerning his "Palace without a Rival."[100] The palace is explicitly described as a cosmic entity, something rooted in primeval creation by the gods: "the everlasting substructure, the eternal foundation; whose plan had been designed from of old, and whose structures have been made beautiful along with the firmament of heaven."[101] Within such royal building accounts (generally in the first person), the "statement of (the builder's) wisdom" regularly occurs. It simply refers to the king's god-given competence or wisdom in building a great "house," its accoutrements and furnishings, or its provisioning gardens and fields. This generic element, the "statement of wisdom," is so prevalent that we might be tempted to dismiss it as a cliché. Instead, its ubiquity indicates its theological importance, not its triviality.

Thus, when Tiglath-pileser III builds a "cedar palace," he does so "with artistic wisdom and extensive skill, which the prince Nudimmud [i.e., Enki/Ea], the sage of the gods, had given me . . . (*i-na uz-ni ni-kil-ti ha-sis-si pal-ke-e ša iš-ru-ka apkal ilāne-meš rubû Nu-dím-mud . . .*").[102] As in Exod 31:3, the deity gives the builder wisdom to build "with wisdom and skill. . . ." Similar is Sennacherib, who in building his colossal lions declares, "I Sennacherib . . . wise in all craftsmanship (*mu-de-e šip-ri*) . . . with the artistic wisdom (*i-na uz-ni ni-kil-ti*) which the noble Nin-igi-kug [*sic* = Ea] had given me, (and) with my own insight (*i-na ši-tul-ti rama-ni-ia*),[103] I counseled deeply with the counsel of my mind (*i-na me-lik ṭe-me-ia*) concerning the matter of carrying out that task. . . ."[104] King Esarhaddon and others use similar stereotyped language.[105]

It is this subsidiary-genre element that appears adapted to Israelite use in Exod 31:3; 35:31; 36:1; 1 Kgs 7:14; Prov 3:19–20; and 24:2–3. The large genre, "royal-building account," with a subsidiary genre element, the "statement of wisdom," has

98. Hurowitz, *I Have Built You an Exalted House*, 236–37.

99. Averbeck, "Sumer," 119.

100. John M. Russell, *Sennacherib's Palace Without Rival at Nineveh* (Chicago: University of Chicago, 1991), esp. 241–62.

101. *ARAB* 2.94, par. 64. Assyrian thinking here reveals the "archetype" and "repetition" thinking made famous by Eliade's *Myth of the Eternal Return*.

102. Tadmor, *Inscriptions of Tiglath-Pileser III*, 172–73 (translation modified).

103. *Šitūltu(m)* is a type of wisdom or skill possessed by an *ummânu*. ABL 1387, 10 (s.v. *šitūltu* in *AHw*).

104. Daniel David Luckenbill, *Sennacherib*, 109. Translation modified. Cf. p. 117: "while Ea provided a spacious womb, and granted (me) artistic skill, the equal of Master Adapa's" (ù dNIN-IGI-KUG [= Ea] *kar-šú rit-pa-šu šun-na-at apkalli A-da-pá pal-ka-a ḫa-sis-su*). See the variant on p. 122: [*i-na*] *uz-ni ni-kil-ti ša ú-šat-li-ma . . .* [*Ea*]). See also p. 133.

105. Borger, *Inschriften*, 82.

its original *Sitz im Leben* in the great courts of Mesopotamia. But in various biblical texts, the larger genre and the subsidiary genre element have undergone some modifications and change of usage. In 1 Kings, we have the closest parallel in form and setting to the ancient Near Eastern royal accounts. However, the account has been changed from the usual first-person declaration that glorifies the king (cf. the ironic usage in Qohelet!) to a third-person report whose focus is not only Solomon, but the Lord whose mastery over cosmos and history is really the point. In both 1 Kings and in Exodus, the "statement of (the builder's) wisdom" is shifted from King Solomon alone, or from Moses, to the actual craftspersons and builders, Hiram and Bezalel. In the final form of the Hebrew Bible, the building account has been subordinated to a much larger composite narrative concerning God's purposes with Israel, an account that ultimately extends from Genesis to the exile in 2 Kings. In the case of Israel's biblical writings, royal aggrandizement is thus subordinated to the person and purposes of the heavenly king, YHWH, so that what may have originally been accounts of royal achievement are set in the context of theological criticism of the great and wise king Solomon. Royal ideology is subordinated to theology.

In the tabernacle account, things are—if possible—even more theological. In terms of macrogenre, the final form of Exodus is akin to many accounts of the new king who vanquishes his enemies, creates or recreates the world (splitting of the Reed Sea), is pronounced king (15:18), institutes law and a new social order (Exodus 19–24), and then proceeds to have his own house built (Exodus 25–40), an act that proclaims his kingship. We see this mythic pattern most famously on the divine level in the *Enūma elish*, which celebrates Marduk's victory over Tiamat and her henchmen, his creation of the world, his acclamation as divine king, his decreeing law, and finally the building of his microcosmic house in Babylon.[106] Crucial here is that the cosmic creation is mirrored in the artificial cosmic mountain, or ziggurat, which is Marduk's house in Babylon. Not without reason is Marduk the son of Enki/Ea, the god of wisdom, and not without reason is he called the *apkal ilī*, the "primal sage of the gods."

CONCLUSIONS

This essay argues that house building is a fundamental metaphoric domain used by ancient Near Eastern societies to express their respective views of human wisdom as rooted in divine wisdom manifest in the ordering and provisioning of the cosmos. Since the composite topos (house building and provisioning + wisdom) is culturally foundational, it is not genre bound, but can be expressed in a variety of forms. Though the topos has its origins in Mesopotamian royal inscriptions, and its first exemplar in

---

106. This "epic" pattern appears also in the Canaanite traditions, and Israel's "Song of the Sea" (Exodus 15) encapsulates it. See Frank M. Cross, *Canaanite Myth and Hebrew Epic: Essays in the History of the Religion of Israel* (Cambridge, Mass.: Harvard University Press, 1973), 112–44.

Gudea's hymns, in the Neo-Assyrian period its most common generic home is in annals of royal *res gestae*. It is adapted in the Bible to express Israel's particular views of tabernacle, temple, creation, and ordinary house building—the latter in wisdom genres that adapt the "statement of the builder's wisdom" to its own purposes. The divine wisdom with its cosmic scope is the basis for the wide variety and scope of human wisdom.

PART FOUR

Biblical Wisdom Literature

Beginnings, Endings, and Life's Necessities in Biblical Wisdom

James L. Crenshaw

Biblical sages devoted an inordinate amount of time observing the mundane activities taking place around them and trying to put their acquired knowledge to optimal use. Even ants were not too tiny to convey significant insights about human productivity, nor drunkards too ludicrous to offer examples of negative behavior. The cyclical events of the seasons and the changing patterns of the weather revealed valuable truths about the workings of a universe believed to be governed by its maker. The sages' task involved the mental processing of information about reality[1] and its analogical application to conduct.[2] They did not always limit their gaze to the ordinary, however, for they occasionally cast their eyes toward the mystery of human origins and final destiny, together with the necessities for life itself.

The Origin of Life

Your hands fashioned and made me
but now you devour me altogether.

---

1. For the processing of information, see James L. Crenshaw, "Qoheleth's Understanding of Intellectual Inquiry," in *Qohelet in the Context of Wisdom* (ed. Anton Schoors; BETL 136; Leuven: Leuven University, 1998), 205–24; idem, *Education in Ancient Israel* (ABRL; New York: Doubleday, 1998); and Michael V. Fox, "The Inner Structure of Qohelet's Thought," in *Qohelet in the Context of Wisdom*, 225–38. Further analysis of epistemology can be found in Peter Machinist, "Fate, *miqreh*, and Reason: Some Reflections on Qohelet and Biblical Thought," in *Solving Riddles and Untying Knots: Biblical, Epigraphic and Semitic Studies in Honor of Jonas C. Greenfield* (ed. Ziony Zevit et al.; Winona Lake, Ind.: Eisenbrauns, 1995), 159–74; and Annette Schellenberg, *Erkenntnis als Problem: Qohelet und die alttestamentliche Diskussion um das menschliche Erkennen* (OBO 188; Göttingen: Vandenhoeck & Ruprecht, 2002).

2. Gerhard von Rad, *Wisdom in Israel* (Nashville: Abingdon, 1972), emphasizes the importance of analogical thinking in the sages' repertoire, while William P. Brown, *Character in Crisis: A Fresh Approach to the Wisdom Literature of the Old Testament* (Grand Rapids: Eerdmans, 1996), stresses the formation of character.

Remember that you made me like clay,
    and will return me to dust.
Did you not pour me out like milk,
    congeal me like cheese?
You clothed me with skin and flesh,
    wove me with bones and sinews.
With life and kindness you endowed me;
    and your solicitude watched over my spirit. (Job 10:8–12)[3]

This reflection about Job's birth is embedded in his third speech. In it, he descends from hymnic praise (9:5–10) to outright accusation of calumny on the deity's part (9:22–24) and imagines that a neutral figure (*môkîaḥ*) would set things right (9:33). Then Job sinks into troubled thoughts about himself as "the work of God's hands" (10:3–22), now despised. The language of crafting underscores the tyranny in the deity's treatment of a lovingly formed object, particularly in light of one of three explanations for idolatry put forth by the author of Wisdom of Solomon.[4] In his view, a craftsman took such pride in what he shaped with his hands that it was set aside for reverential awe (Wis 14:18–20).

It seems to Job that the deity's intimate knowledge of him serves a malicious purpose, enabling the hunter to kill his prey. Having destroyed the moral order, the arbiter of justice orchestrates uncontrolled violence against an innocent victim who must plead for mercy, an intolerable perversion of justice. The language of parody predominates here, with Job mocking the traditional notion that divine intimacy implies providential care. Such thoughts do not stop short of imagining the reversal of the original creative act, a return to primordial chaos like that envisioned by Jeremiah (4:23–26). The language of paradox occurs as well, for Job ponders an eerie world in which darkness shines. Such a world would seem to encourage a longing for death, as in Job's initial lament in chap. 3, but the forensic metaphor that Job now embraces drives out such thoughts and equips him with an unprecedented boldness that demands a fair trial.

The extraordinary picture of personal origin in 10:8–12 returns to the theme enunciated in 10:3, humankind as the work of divine hands. The language suggests toil, thereby throwing in relief the contrast between fashioning and destroying in 10:8. The two verbs connoting Job's origin (*ʿśh* and *ʿśh*)[5] are matched by a single verb

---

3. Translations in this article are by the author unless otherwise indicated.

4. Maurice Gilbert, *La Critique des dieux dans le livre de la Sagesse* (AnBib 53; Rome: Pontifical Biblical Institute, 1973), offers a thorough analysis of the attitude to idolatry in Wisdom of Solomon. Along with the worship of distant emperors and grief over a dead son, pride in artistic craft completes the three explanations for worshiping something finite. John F. Kutsko, *Between Heaven and Earth: Divine Presence and Absence in the Book of Ezekiel* (Biblical and Judaic Studies from the University of California, San Diego 7; Winona Lake, Ind.: Eisenbrauns, 2000), relates theodicy and the prophetic understanding of the worship of "non-gods."

5. J. Vollmer, "עשׂה, *ʿśh*, to make, do," *TLOT*, 2:944–51.

signifying destruction (*bl'*). With feigned deference, Job implores God to remember that his own beginning echoes the first fashioning of humankind, with the deity's subsequent pronouncement of destiny: "You are dust, and to dust you will return." The potter's exceptional contribution to daily existence and the relationship between potter and clay provided a natural image for the mystery of birth. It did not convey the sensual aspects related to conception, however; for this idea, Job alludes to the result of ejaculation, the pouring out of the substance of lifelike milk and its mixture with an "unknown" in the womb (10:10). For this coming together of life's ingredients, he uses the familiar concept of congealing cheese (cf. Wis 7:2, the mixing of semen with the woman's bodily fluid).[6] Reaching into another realm of daily life, Job likens the development of the fetus within the mother's womb to the act of weaving. He is clothed with skin and flesh, while bones and sinews are woven together (*skk*) like an intricate garment (10:11).[7] This tender care was extended (Job does not say how long) in order to preserve breath by solicitous care (*ḥayyîm* and *ḥesed*). The irony could hardly be greater. The loving care expended on knitting together the skeletal structure has been replaced by uncontrolled aggression aimed at destroying Job.

The similarities between Job 10:8–12 and Ps 139:13–18 have long been recognized, in general content if not in tone.

> Indeed,[8] you created my conscience,[9]
> fashioned[10] me in my mother's womb.
> I praise you, for I am awesomely and wondrously made.
> Wonderful are your works,
> which I know well.
> My body was not hidden from you,
> when I was fashioned secretly,
> woven together in earth's recesses.
> Your eyes beheld my unformed substance;[11]
> all of its parts were recorded in your book.[12]
> In time they were formed,
> and not one of them [had existed].
> How precious to me are your thoughts, God,
> their number, how great.

---

6. Carol A. Newsom, "The Book of Job," *NIB*, 4:414, refers to Édouard Dhorme, *A Commentary on the Book of Job* (London: Nelson, 1967), 149–50, for parallels from later literature.

7. Samson's response to Delilah's badgering in Judg 16:13 employs an imperfect form of *'ārag* together with a noun from *nāsak* II with the meaning "web." The imperfect verbal form in Job 10:11 to indicate intricate weaving is from *sākak*.

8. The initial *kî* is taken as emphatic here.

9. Literally, "kidneys."

10. The verb is *tĕsukkēnî*, as in Job 10:11 (*tĕsōkĕkēnî*).

11. This word *golmî* ("embryo") evoked considerable speculation in later Judaism.

12. On this idea, see Shalom M. Paul, "Heavenly Tablets and the Book of Life," *JANESCU* 5 (1973): 345–53.

> I count them—more than the sand;
> I stop—I am still with you. (Ps 139:13–18)

The poem that has this acknowledgment of the awesome product of divine creativity begins with praise (vv. 1–6) and ends with supplication (vv. 23–24). It also contains a puzzling query about escaping from such complete divine surveillance (vv. 7–12) and a cry for the extirpation of personal enemies, whom the psalmist considers enemies of the deity too (vv. 19–22). This combination of themes is difficult to categorize beyond meditative reflection in the guise of a legal plea for divine judgment.

The initial section, marked by the language of intimacy, an "I" addressing a divine "You," explores the extent of Yahweh's knowledge of the psalmist. Traditional language indicates intellectual probing that exposes the inner being of the poet, whose every act and thought are fully known. Even the words that express this marvel are known before their articulation, the psalmist insists. Does such divine searching of every thought and deed limit human freedom and become oppressive in the long run?[13] Verse 5 seems to suggest a certain feeling of unease when asserting that the deity hedges the psalmist in "front and back," laying a hand on him. Is the touch a consoling one, like that alluded to in Ps 73:23 ("But I am always with you; you hold my right hand"),[14] or an intrusive invasion of privacy? The next verse may support either interpretation: (1) the mystery is wonderful, like the deity to whom the epithet "worker of wonders" is applied, or (2) such awesome knowledge is more than the psalmist can endure (*lō' 'ūkal lāh*).[15]

The question that introduces the next section appears to support the second interpretation, for why would a contented worshiper ponder the possibility of fleeing from the divine presence? Neither height nor depth offers any respite. The same is true for east and west, except that on this journey with the wings of dawn to the western horizon, Yahweh's guiding hand holds the psalmist securely. Here the language echoes the consolation celebrated in Ps 73:23. That comforting thought quickly vanishes, to be replaced by words about hiding under cover of darkness, a familiar idea that is usually associated with practical atheists in the Psalter.[16] Unfortunately, for one who is inclined to use darkness as a shield from divine observation, day and night are alike to Yahweh, or so the psalmist thinks.

---

13. Samuel Terrien, *The Psalms: Strophic Structure and Theological Commentary* (Grand Rapids: Eerdmans, 2003), 876–78. "The poet rebels against a doting father who dictates every move and word of his adored child. Now surprise! This harassed child asks for more 'divine examination, scrutiny, and search'" (p. 878).

14. James L. Crenshaw, *The Psalms: An Introduction* (Grand Rapids: Eerdmans, 2001), 109–27.

15. Similar language is used in Agur's opening remarks (Prov 30:1) to indicate incapacity, and in Jeremiah's lament in 20:7 where it lacks the negation because the referent is Yahweh. The result is the same—human impotence.

16. Three psalms, 10, 14, and 54, stand out as expressions of this attitude, which is linked with fools. I treat each of these psalms in *Defending God: Biblical Responses to the Problem of Evil* (New York: Oxford University Press, 2005).

The psalmist's imagination falls short of the hypothetical comments that Amos attributes to Yahweh (Amos 9:2–4). In this prophetic text, sinners hoping to escape divine punishment are said to be engaged in a futile exercise, despite their flight to Sheol or the heavens, to remote Carmel or further west into the sea, or to far-away exile. Even were they able to hide in the depths of the sea, Yahweh exclaims, a serpent awaits the divine command. Similarly, a sword is prepared to do the deity's will in exile. The oracle of doom sounds the death knell: "My eye is fixed on them for harm, not good."[17]

The psalmist's thoughts about his origin oscillate between self-praise and exaltation of the deity, who is called El here in contrast to Yahweh in Ps 139:1, 4, and 21. A hint of hubris has been detected in the language of ascent into heaven,[18] an honor previously reserved for exceptional people such as Enoch[19] and Elijah and later extended more broadly to the faithful in Pss 49:16 and 73:24. In apocalyptic texts,[20] certain chosen ones are taken on a journey into heaven but make the return trip carrying with them special knowledge about the mysteries of the world (contrast, however, Prov 30:4).[21]

Verse 13 opens with an emphatic *kî* (indeed), although it is possible to understand the particle as a justification for the previous statement that Yahweh's vision penetrates darkness ("For you created my kidneys"). When *kilyōtāy* is combined with *lēb*,

---

17. Shalom M. Paul, *Amos* (Hermeneia; Minneapolis: Fortress, 1991), 277, notes the presence of pentads here (five conditional sentences highlighted by a fivefold repetition of *miššām* "from there") and in the earlier refrain, *wělō' šabtem 'ādai ne'um YHWH* (4:6–11), and five visions. Paul's exemplary treatment of Amos 9:2–4 draws on ancient Near Eastern parallels while being attentive to literary and theological features of the Hebrew text.

18. Terrien, *The Psalms*, 877. He writes, "Nevertheless, the poet does not stumble under the threat of metaphysical hubris." Elsewhere Terrien admires this poet's "skill, finesse, and force, as if he were a religious acrobat who dances on the high wire without a safety net" while exclaiming, "All my ways are known to thee, Lord" (p. 879).

19. James C. VanderKam, *Enoch: A Man for All Generations* (Columbia: University of South Carolina Press, 1995).

20. John J. Collins, *The Apocalyptic Imagination: An Introduction to the Jewish Matrix of Christianity* (2d ed.; New York: Crossroad, 1998); and idem, "Early Jewish Apocalypticism," *ABD*, 1:281–88.

21. Raymond C. Van Leeuwen, "The Background to Proverbs 30:4aα," in *Wisdom, You Are My Sister: Studies in Honor of Roland E. Murphy, O. Carm., on the Occasion of His Eightieth Birthday* (ed. Michael L. Barré, S.S.; CBQMS 29; Washington, D.C.: Catholic Biblical Association, 1995), 102–21. For the larger text Prov 30:1–14, see James L. Crenshaw, "Clanging Symbols," in *Justice and the Holy* (ed. D. A. Knight and P. J. Paris; Philadelphia: Fortress, 1989), 51–64; repr. in *Urgent Advice and Probing Questions: Collected Writings on Old Testament Wisdom* (Macon, Ga.: Mercer University, 1995), 371–82. Karel van der Toorn, "Sources in Heaven: Revelation as a Scholarly Construct in Second Temple Judaism," in *Kein Land für sich allein: Studien zum Kulturkontakt in Kanaan, Israel/Palästina und Ebirnâri für Manfred Weippert zum 65. Geburtstag* (ed. Ulrich Hübner and Ernst Axel Knauf; OBO 186; Göttingen: Vandenhoeck & Ruprecht, 2002), 265–77, stresses the emergence of the concept of revelation to replace earlier human wisdom in Mesopotamia and Israel. He views the first-millennium version of the Myth of Adapa in this light, for Adapa returned from heaven with the revealed secrets of heaven, knowledge hidden from ordinary mortals (p. 274).

the two nouns indicate the emotions and intellect respectively.[22] The personal pronoun *'attāh* gives added specification to the verb *qānîtā*, in which one hears an echo of Deut 32:6b ("Is he not your father who created you [*qāneka*]; he formed [*'ăśĕkā*] and established you?"). The psalmist's choice of the verb *tĕsukkēnî* (Ps 139:13) to convey the interweaving of bodily parts in the mother's womb suggests loving attention and consummate skill. The proper response to such creative activity finds expression in a single word, *'ôdĕkā* ("I praise you"). The reason: "for I am wondrously made—awesome." The psalmist dares to include himself in El's *ma'ăśîm*, of which he claims intimate knowledge (*wĕnapšî yōda'at mĕ'ōd*). The doubling of words from the roots *pl'* and *nr'*, which normally indicate Yahweh's mighty actions and their awe-inspiring effect, reinforces the exalted assessment of a mere mortal and rivals the praise in Psalm 8. Returning to the notion of concealment, he asserts that El was equally familiar with the fetus when fashioning it in secret, weaving together its separate parts in earth's depths.

This allusion to the myth of mother earth leads naturally to traditional lore about divine scribal activity, a fixing of the destiny of all creatures, which then evokes the revered story about the divine promise of progeny to Abraham in Genesis 15. It seems that by alluding to Abraham and Moses the poet wishes to situate his own extraordinary origin within Israel's sacred history. Such thoughts about divine priorities (*rā'šêhem*) are believed to be as precious as they are innumerable. The psalmist imagines that in the act of counting he runs out of numbers. One thing is constant, however; he does not believe that he has reached the end of divine immediacy.[23]

> Just as you cannot know the manner of the wind—like bones in the womb of a pregnant woman—so you cannot know the deity's work who makes everything. (Eccl 11:5)

Although many interpreters emend the text to read "in the bones" and understand the reference to be the entering of the life breath into the fetus, there is no need to alter the preserved text. Qoheleth observes that our inability to understand how the wind causes movement in the branches of a tree is exactly like our ignorance about the power that enables a fetus to move about inside the womb. Equally obscure, he remarks, is the deity's activity, although everything is the direct result of a divine act.[24]

---

22. F. Stolz, "לב, *lēb*, heart," *TLOT*, 2:638–42. "In addition to *kābēd* 'liver' (→ *kbd*), particular reference should be made to *kĕlāyôt* 'kidneys' which often parallels the 'heart,' indicating the most private, hidden being of a person, accessible only to God . . ."(p. 640).

23. Amos Hakham, *The Bible, Psalms with The Jerusalem Commentary* (Jerusalem: Mosad Harav Kook, 2003), 3:400–411, is a perceptive analysis of the entire psalm.

24. James L. Crenshaw, "From the Mundane to the Sublime (Reflections on Qoh 11:1–8)," *From Babel to Babylon: Essays on Biblical History and Literature in Honour of Brian Peckham* (ed. Joyce Rilett Wood, John E. Harvey, and Mark Leuchter; New York and London: T & T Clark, 2006), 301–19. The midrash *Qoheleth Rabbah* includes this mystery of birth in the seven great mysteries. The others are the day of one's death, the timing of the messianic consolation, the profundity of divine judgment, the source from which one will profit, the precise thought or feeling in a friend's heart, and the exact time that the kingdom of Edom (= Rome) will fall.

I do not know how you came into being in my womb.
It was not I who gave you life and breath, nor I who
set in order the elements within each of you. Therefore
the Creator of the world, who shaped the beginnings of man
and devised the origin of all things, will in his
mercy give life and breath back to you again, since
you now forget yourselves for the sake of his laws,
(2 Macc 7:20–23, RSV)

The impassioned speech of this mother of seven martyrs is said to have fueled a woman's reason with a man's courage, but the contrast with sapiential precedent could hardly be greater. Here the mother draws on familiar concepts about the deity's role in the mystery of birth as the basis for confidence in the ultimate rectification of gross injustice. The same power that originated life can, in her view, give it back as reward for faithfully observing the Torah. Belief in divine bestowal of life now functions as theodicy.[25] How different this is from 4 Macc 2:21–22, which stresses the enthronement of the intellect amid the senses as the essential gift bestowed at birth![26]

THE END

Speculation about life's termination occupied the thought of the sages primarily as a result of the collapse of belief in a moral order.[27] Their thoughts were by no means unified, ranging from the assertion that death was both natural and final to the conviction that humankind possesses an immortal soul. A mediating position—that no one knows whether the human spirit ascends, in contrast to a descending animal spirit—characterized the view of Qoheleth, whose preoccupation with death was nearly obsessive.[28]

In Job's view, life fades and withers like a flower, vanishing like a shadow (Job 14:2), whereas a tree can sprout new growth after being cut down (14:7). Once a

---

25. Antti Laato and Johannes C. de Moor, eds., *Theodicy in the World of the Bible* (Leiden: Brill, 2003); and James L. Crenshaw, *Defending God*; and idem, "Theodicy in the Book of the Twelve," 175–91, in *Thematic Threads in the Book of the Twelve* (ed. Paul L. Redditt and Aaron Schart; BZAW 325; Berlin: de Gruyter, 2003) attest the powerful attraction of this vexing problem, brought to public attention once more by the devastating tsunami of December 2004.

26. Hugh Anderson, "4 Maccabees," *OTP*, 2:531–64. Strongly influenced by Stoic philosophers, the author of 4 Maccabees departs from them in the belief that reason controls the passions instead of extirpating them (see note e on p. 546).

27. No one has emphasized the collapse of belief in order throughout the ancient Near East as decisively as Hans Heinrich Schmid, *Wesen und Geschichte der Weisheit* (BZAW 101; Berlin: Töpelmann, 1966). Questioning the significance of order is Roland E. Murphy, on which see James L. Crenshaw, "Murphy's Axiom: Every Gnomic Saying Needs a Balancing Corrective," in *Urgent Advice and Probing Questions*, 344–54.

28. James L. Crenshaw, "The Shadow of Death in Qoheleth," in *Urgent Advice and Probing Questions*, 573–85; and Shannon Burkes, *Death in Qoheleth and Egyptian Biographies of the Late Period* (SBLDS 170; Atlanta: Society of Biblical Literature, 1999).

person succumbs to death, there is no rising until the heavens are no more (14:12). All the more perplexing, Job thinks, is the deity's relentless destruction of hope, which he compares to water wearing away rocks and eroding the landscape (14:18–19).[29] The erosion of hope has taken effect in Qoheleth, whose agnostic position is summed up in his final words: "Dust returns to earth as it was, and the life breath returns to God who gave it" (Eccl 12:7). The words that follow prevent a positive reading of the second colon: "Utter futility, said Qoheleth; everything is futile" (12:8). Indeed, the graphic depiction of the aging process, set over against the encouragement to make the most of youth, emphasizes death's finality by the choice of images that signal the end: the snapping of the silver cord, breaking of the golden bowl, and smashing of the jug at the cistern (12:6). These irreversible moments inaugurate the journey to an eternal abode.

Ben Sira minces no words when declaring that death, the decree for all, is final (Sir 34:7); he, too, uses the symbol of a tree to convey his thought that when old leaves are shed new ones take their place. So one person dies and another is born, continuing the cycle of life. More importantly, he insists, there is a good death just as there is an unwelcome one, the latter coming when one is prosperous and healthy (41:1–4). Curiously, Ben Sira preserves the tradition that Elijah resuscitated a corpse (48:5), but temporary restoration of life was entirely different from the concept of resurrection that emerged shortly after Ben Sira.[30]

The Hellenistic environment that may have influenced the views of death in Qoheleth and Ben Sira, even if negatively,[31] was the formative influence on the author of Wisdom of Solomon.[32] In his opinion, the righteous dead are at peace, possessing the hope of immortality (3:3–4).[33] Adopting the persona of Solomon, the author claims to have been endowed with a good soul and an undefiled body (8:19–20). In this author's view, death marks the transition to an everlasting existence with God. Whether one understands death as final or as transitional, it inevitably looms before

---

29. James L. Crenshaw, "Flirting with the Language of Prayer (Job 14:13–17)," in *Worship and the Hebrew Bible: Essays in Honor of John T. Willis* (ed. M. Patrick Graham et al.; JSOT 284; Sheffield: Sheffield Academic Press, 1999), 110–23

30. James L. Crenshaw, "Love Is Stronger Than Death (Intimations of Life Beyond the Grave)," in *Resurrection: The Origin and Future of a Biblical Doctrine* (ed. James Charlesworth; New York and London: T & T Clark, 2006), 53–78.

31. Martin Hengel, *Judaism and Hellenism* (Philadelphia: Fortress, 1974), 107–53; Otto Kaiser, *Gottes und der Menschen Weisheit: Gesammelte Aufsätze* (BZAW 261; Berlin: de Gruyter, 1998); S. L. Mattila, "Ben Sira and the Stoics: A Re-examination of the Evidence," *JBL* 119 (2000): 473–501; U. Wicke-Reuter, *Göttliche Providenz und menschliche Verantwortung bei Ben Sira und in der Frühen Stoa* (BZAW 298; Berlin: de Gruyter, 2000); and Reinhold Bohlen, "Kohelet im Kontext hellenistischer Kultur," in *Das Buch Kohelet: Studien zur Kultur, Geschichte, Rezeption, und Theologie* (ed. L. Schwienhorst-Schönberger; BZAW 254; Berlin: de Gruyter, 1997), 249–73.

32. David Winston, *The Wisdom of Solomon* (AB 43; Garden City, N.Y.: Doubleday, 1979).

33. Michael Kolarcik, *The Ambiguity of Death in the Book of Wisdom 1–6: A Study of Literary Structure and Interpretation* (AnBib 127; Rome: Pontifical Biblical Institute, 1991).

one as a reminder that choices must be made about priorities. In the face of death, what are life's essentials?

THE NECESSITIES OF LIFE

archē zoēs hydōr, kai artos, kai himation, kai oikos kalypton archēmosynēn. (Sir 29:21)

The principle things of life are water, bread, clothing, and a house to cover one's nakedness.

ṭwb lṭ]wb ḥlq mr'š / kn lr'ym ṭwb wr'
[r'š k]l [ṣrk lḥym] 'dm mym / w'š wbrzl wmlḥ
[ḥlb ḥṭh ḥ]lb wdbš / dm 'nb yšhr wbgd
kl [ṭwb lṭwb]ym yyṭybw / kn lr'ym lr'h nhpkw.[34] (Sir 39:25–27)

From the beginning he (God) has apportioned good things for the
     virtuous,
        similarly for the wicked, good and bad things.
The essentials of every human need are water,
        fire, iron, salt,
        the marrow of wheat, milk, honey,
        blood of the grape, oil, and clothing.
All these become good for the virtuous,
        just as they are turned into bad things for the wicked.

In these two texts, Ben Sira offers rather different responses to the same unstated question: On what does human life depend? The interpreter gains little from dwelling on the author's inconsistency or even from detecting signs of sociological advancement on Ben Sira's part, as if he mirrors Israel's cultural development from village life to an urban setting.[35] Perhaps a better approach is to recognize the two distinct aims indicated by the larger contexts. The Spartan list of only four basic needs is set within a discussion of social responsibility to offer assistance to members of the community who fall on hard times, whereas the expansive cataloging of life's fundamental needs functions as theodicy.[36]

---

34. I follow the text as produced in Pancratius C. Beentjes, *The Book of Ben Sira in Hebrew: A Text Edition of All Extant Hebrew Manuscripts and Synopsis of all Parallel Hebrew Ben Sira Texts* (Leiden: Brill, 1997).

35. Georg Sauer, *Jesus Sirach/Ben Sira* (ATD Apokryphen Band 1; Göttingen: Vandenhoeck & Ruprecht, 2000), writes: "Eine kleine Kulturgeschichte kann an dieser Aufzählung abgelesen werden, vgl. auch Sir 29, 21 und Dtn 32:13f." (p. 274).

36. Pancratius C. Beentjes, "Theodicy in the Wisdom of Ben Sira," in *Theodicy in the World of the Bible*, 509–24, and John J. Collins, *Jewish Wisdom in the Hellenistic Age* (OTL; Louisville: Westminster,

In the first instance, Ben Sira understands that in the face of widespread hunger, regardless of its particular expression, life can be sustained by bread and water for nurture and clothing and shelter for protection from the elements and from the shame of uncovering one's nakedness to one and all. Everything beyond these four things is disposable property and therefore constitutes a fund into which one can dip to provide charitable assistance. Because of his astute study of human nature, Ben Sira realizes that lending money has undesirable features; nevertheless, he advocates compassionate action regardless of these possible consequences. By such acts of kindness to the poor, he believes, one can deposit assets in a heavenly treasury on which to draw when the need arises. Although Ben Sira recognizes that entering into relationships in which one provides surety for another person can have disastrous consequences, he still recommends compassion, but with open eyes. Above all, he warns, a person should not become dependent on others for subsistence, for such parasitic existence robs one of dignity.

In the second instance, Ben Sira reflects on divine largesse, which he considers to be far from niggardly. Blessings abound, he thinks, even when one restricts thought to the essentials of life. Possibly influenced by Greek philosophical theodicies based on the functional duality of opposites in nature,[37] he argues that various things are neutral until directed at specific persons, when they become either beneficial to the good or detrimental to the health of the wicked. In this context, Ben Sira draws on familiar tradition about a promised land of milk and honey, as well as lavish descriptions of Canaan as a place of abundant grain, oil, and wine.[38] In addition, he mentions fire, iron, and salt—the last to enhance flavor; the second to improve the quality of life through tools and weapons; and the first as essential to cooking and to forge implements of agriculture and of warfare. Naturally, Ben Sira includes water, bread, and clothing in this longer list but curiously omits shelter.

Nature's unruly forces (such as fire, hail, famine, and pestilence) as well as dangerous creatures (Ben Sira mentions wild beasts, scorpions, and vipers) function in this well-ordered universe to punish the wicked, according to this theodicy. Ben Sira trusts his reasoning so much that he puts it in writing,[39] having thoroughly examined its logic. He concludes: *m'śh 'l klm ṭwbym lkl ṣwrk b'tw yspwq* ("God's works—all of them—are good; he supplies all your needs in their times" [Sir 39:33]). It follows that anyone who makes superficial distinctions between good and bad things per se does not reckon with the reality that everything is appropriate for its purpose. In this judg-

---

1997), 80–96, supplement my earlier article, "The Problem of Theodicy in Sirach: On Human Bondage," *JBL* 94 (1975): 49–64; repr. in *Urgent Advice and Probing Questions*, 155–74.

37. Patrick W. Skehan and Alexander A. DiLella, *The Wisdom of Ben Sira* (AB 39; New York: Doubleday, 1987), 457–61.

38. Skehan and DiLella list the following biblical references, among others: Gen 49:11 (grain and wine); Hos 2:10; Jer 31:12; Neh 10:38 [39] (oil); Exod 3:8; 13:5; 33:3; Lev 20:24 (milk and honey).

39. On writing as enculturation, see David M. Carr, *Writing on the Tablet of the Heart: Origins of Scripture and Literature* (New York: Oxford University Press, 2005).

ment, Ben Sira concurs with Qoheleth's sentiment in Eccl 3:11 (*'et-hakkōl 'āśāh yāpeh be'ittô*, "He made everything appropriate for its purpose"). Everything has its special time, that is, even if the two thinkers differed radically about whether or not humans can put such knowledge to good use.

In both versions of life's necessities, water takes precedence, perhaps because bread, the other ingredient that is absolutely essential, depends on it. Fire assumes the second position in the longer account, probably because of its role in transforming grain into bread. In neither list does meat appear, a noteworthy departure from Deut 32:13–14.

> He made him [Israel] ride on the top of the earth
> so that he feasted on the produce of the field.
> He made him suck honey from a crag
> and oil from a flinty rock;
> Curds from cattle and goat's milk,
> with fat lambs;
> Rams from Bashan and he-goats,
> with the best wheat;
> you would drink wine, the blood of the grape.

In the judgment of the poet, however, Yahweh's lavish provision failed to generate gratitude, yielding instead an arrogance that found expression in idolatry. The danger inherent to riches was not foreign to the author of the only prayer in the Book of Proverbs. Here one reads, "Two things I ask from you; do not withhold them from me before I die. Emptiness and lying words keep far from me; do not give me poverty or riches but break off for me a portion of bread, lest I be sated and deny, saying 'Who is Yahweh?' or lest being poor I steal and sully the name of my God" (Prov 30:7–9).[40]

Ben Sira's shorter version of life's essentials has been taken as endorsing simple values associated with working the soil, but it is hardly that, for in his hierarchy of sociological status sages rank just behind rulers, priests, and possibly merchants.[41] The later author of *Pirqe Abot* (*m. 'Abot* 2:7) comes close to stating a preference for austere existence, however, when listing the dangers of economic prosperity such as gluttony, worry over theft, serial polygamy leading to witchcraft, and anxiety brought on by a house full of servants. Over against these products of abundance, he names the benefits of Torah, study, counsel, and deeds of charity. They are, respectively, life, wisdom, understanding, and peace.

---

40. James L. Crenshaw, "The Restraint of Reason, the Humility of Prayer," in *Urgent Advice and Probing Questions*, 206–21, examines the place of prayer in sapiential literature.

41. Oda Wischmeyer, *Die Kultur des Buches Jesus Sirach* (BZNW 77; Berlin: de Gruyter, 1994).

> Go, eat your bread joyfully and drink your wine merrily, for the deity has already approved your action. Let your clothes be white at all times, and do not let your head lack oil. Enjoy life with the woman you love all the days of your brief existence that he has granted you under the sun—all your brief days, for that is your portion in life and in your toil at which you labor under the sun. (Eccl 9:7–9)

Although lacking Ben Sira's language about the essentials of life, Qoheleth's exhortation, strikingly similar to Siduri's advice to Gilgamesh,[42] approximates the short version discussed above. Life's injustices, together with its brevity, lend urgency to conduct that will maximize enjoyment, Qoheleth concludes. His understanding of life's essentials includes bread, drink, and clothing, but also soothing ointment and companionship.[43] In this text, we hear an echo of the invitation tendered by Wisdom in Prov 9:5. Having slaughtered her meat and having mixed drinks for her guests, she issues the following invitation: "Come, eat my food (literally, "bread") and drink my mixed wine." Not to be undone, Folly alludes to bread and water in a masterfully crafted seduction ("Stolen water is sweet, and bread eaten clandestinely is tasty" [Prov 9:17]). In yet another context, Qoheleth adds money to the other two necessities, bread and wine ("For laughter they prepare bread, and wine makes life joyful, but money answers everything" [Eccl 10:19]).[44]

The following proverb appears in a context dealing with survival, which depends in this case on the condition of a small flock of sheep and goats.

> Lambs are for clothing, and he-goats for the price of a field; goats' milk is adequate for your food—for the food of your house and the subsistence of your maidens. (Prov 27:26–27)

The proverb urges one to take special care of these precious commodities, for on their well-being the survival of the family depends. Of what does that consist? Just two things: food and clothing; or, at most, three, because a field is essential for the animals' existence and ultimately for their owners' as well.

If it is true that "man does not live by bread alone," the door swings open for additional necessities. The first to enter, according to Prov 1:7, is the fear of Yahweh, the

---

42. The remarkable similarities between the two texts could be explained without reference to literary influence. It would then be an instance of polygenesis, the spontaneous emergence of similar ideas in separate locations. It is much more likely, however, that the story about Gilgamesh was known to Qoheleth, given its wide distribution in the ancient Near East.

43. The irony of Qoheleth's recognition of the necessity of companionship to the good life, insofar as it could be achieved, should not escape notice, particularly in light of his egoism, on which Peter Höffken has written astutely ("Das Ego des Weisen," TZ 4 [1985]: 121–35).

44. Qoheleth's use of the verb ʿānāh in different senses has made it difficult to understand one verse in particular, 5:19. Does maʿāneh imply affliction, preoccupation, or answer? Norbert Lohfink, "Qoheleth 5:17–19—Revelation by Joy," CBQ 52 (1990): 625–35; and Ludger Schwienhorst-Schönberger, "Gottes Antwort in der Freude: Zur Theologie göttlicher Gegenwart im Buch Kohelet," Bibel und Kirche 54 (1999): 156–63, prefer the last meaning, thus a positive interpretation of the text.

rēʾšît (first principle) of knowledge. Religious devotion, that is, lies at the heart of the intellectual enterprise. In that spirit, the epilogist concludes the Book of Ecclesiastes by observing that everything has been heard and by proclaiming the end of the matter[45] to be "Fear God and keep his commandments" (Eccl 12:13). With the dual sense of *rēʾšît* above (first principle and beginning), we return to the idea with which this discussion began, but now in the context of endings.[46]

---

45. Avi Hurvitz, "רֹאשׁ־דָּבָר and סוֹף־דָּבָר: Reflexes of Two Scribal Terms Imported into Biblical Hebrew from the Imperial Aramaic Formulary," in *Hamlet on a Hill: Semitic and Greek Studies Presented to Professor T. Muraoka on the Occasion of his Sixty-Fifth Birthday*, 281–86 (ed. M. F. J. Baasten and W. Th. Van Peursen; OLA 118; Leuven: Peeters, 2003), writes that *rōʾš* and *sôp* represent semantic mirror images. In Qoheleth and Psalm 119 *rōʾš-dābār* and *sôp-dābār* denote "the beginning of the matter" and "the end of the matter," not the scribal "beginning/end of a [written] word (=text)."

46. One could profitably extend this discussion of beginnings and endings to the difficult problem of delineating textual units, as well as to prologues, epilogues, and thematic statements. Norbert Lohfink, "Jeder Weisheitslehre Quintessenz. Zu Koh 12, 13," in *Auf den Spuren der schriftgelehrten Weisen: Festschrift für Johannes Marböck* (ed. Irmtraud Fischer et al.; BZAW 331; Berlin: de Gruyter, 2003), 195–205; and idem, "Zu einigen Satzeröffnungen im Epilog des Koheletbuches," in *"Jedes Ding hat seine Zeit . . ."* (ed. A. A. Diesel et al.; BZAW 241; Berlin: de Gruyter, 1996), 131–47, has initiated such an investigation. The language of origins attributed to Wisdom in Prov 8:22–31 could also be studied fruitfully in this connection, but that would extend the scope of this paper to an unacceptable length. The initiative for such analysis has been taken by Michaela Bauks and Gerlinde Baumann, "Im Anfang war . . . ? Gen 1,1ff und Prov 8, 22–31 in Vergleich," *BN* 71 (1994): 24–53.

Contributors

Paul-Alain Beaulieu
Associate Professor of Assyriology, University of Toronto.

Richard J. Clifford
Professor of Old Testament, Weston Jesuit School of Theology

James L. Crenshaw
Robert L. Flowers Professor of Old Testament, Duke University Divinity School

Edward Greenstein
Professor of Bible, Bar-Ilan University, Ramat Gan

Victor Avigdor Hurowitz
Professor, Department of Bible and Ancient Near Eastern Studies, Ben-Gurion University of the Negev

Karel van der Toorn
President of the University of Amsterdam and Professor of the Religions of Antiquity

Raymond C. Van Leeuwen
Professor of Biblical Studies, Eastern University

Index of Ancient Documents

Hebrew Bible
Hebrew Bible citations follow MT numbering

GENESIS
1:1–2:3   76
2:22   73
49:1   40

EXODUS
31:3   84, 85 n.89, 88
35:25–26   85
40:34–35   77

DEUTERONOMY
32:13–14   103

JUDGES
14:16–17   47

1 KINGS
5   84
7:14   85
8:1–5   72, 85
8:11   77
10:4–8,23–24   75

ISAIAH
6   46
6:13   84
40:12   77
66:1–2   77

JEREMIAH
5:22   70
10:12   84

EZEKIEL
36:1   84

MICAH
7:5   47

PSALMS
49   45, 49, 50
65:10–14   70
73:23   96
74:15   78 n.53
104   70, 72 n.26, 77 n.50, 78 n.53
139:13–18   95–98

JOB   4, 7, 44
3:14–15   75
10:8–12   93–94
38   77
38:8a, 10–11   70

PROVERBS   33 n.4, 37 n.2, 44, 45
1:5–11   47
1:13   80
1:8–19   42 n.17
1:20–33   79
2:9   44
3:19–20   70, 77, 78 n.54, 79, 80, 83, 84, 85 n.89, 86 n.91, 87, 88
5:15–20   70
6:26–35   42 n.17
8:1–36   79, 86 n.93
8:24, 27–29   70
9:1–6   72, 79, 80, 86 n.93
10:11   47
11:12   48
13:14a   70

Proverbs (*continued*)
15:20	47
20:18	47
20:27	49
22:17–24:22	44
23:29–35	46
24:3–4	50, 77–80, 82, 84, 86 n.91, 87
24:6	47
25–29	44
27:23–26	50, 104
29:21	47
30:4	33 n.3
30:7–9	103
30:7–33	44
31	85
31:4–7	46

ECCLESIASTES
	4, 37 n.2, 38, 44, 45, 55–65
1:10	45
1:16	58
1:17	61
2:3	63
2:4	75
2:5–6	70
2:12	63
2:13–14	64
2:18–21	50
3	58
3:9	57
3:11	103
4:2	57
4:6	63
4:12	63
4:8–5:7	50
4:9–12	46
5:11	64
6:3	64
7:2–4	46
7:3	61,63
7:23–24	57
7:26	57
8:14	57
9:4	64
9:7–9	104
9:10	50
11:1–6	50, 98

12:7	45 n.22
12:13	105

2 CHRONICLES
2	84 n.86

Deuterocanonical Texts

SIRACH
24	86
29:21	101
39:25–27	101

WISDOM OF SOLOMON
7–9	86
9:8–12	82

2 MACCABEES
7:20–23	99

Sumerian

DEATH OF GILGAMESH	5, 7

ENKI AND THE WORLD ORDER	68, 69 n.12, 70

ERIDU GENESIS (*see* SUMERIAN FLOOD STORY)

INSTRUCTIONS OF SHURUPPAK	xii, xiii, 4 n.2, 5, 6,17, 42, 43, 44, 46, 48

INSTRUCTIONS OF UR–NINURTA	6 n.10, 17

A MAN AND HIS GOD	xii, xiii, 8

ŠULGI HYMNS	83 n.76

SUMERIAN FLOOD STORY	5, 70 n.18

Akkadian

ADAPA	46, 88 n.104, 97 n.21

ADVICE TO A PRINCE	xii, xiii, 17

ASSURBANIPAL'S INSTALLATION SPEECH
ARAB 2.769 80

BABYLONIAN THEODICY
xii, xiii 4, 8, 9, 11, 13, 43

BIT MĒSERI 22

CATALOG OF TEXTS AND AUTHORS
9 n.20, 12, 13, 15, 16, 21 n.2

COMPENDIUM OF THE EXORCIST 12 n.28

COUNSELS OF WISDOM
xii, xiii, 33 n.4, 42, 43

DIAGNOSTIC HANDBOOK 10 n.22, 12, 13

DIALOGUE BETWEEN A MAN AND
HIS GOD xiii, 8

DIALOGUE BETWEEN A MASTER AND
HIS SERVANT (see DIALOGUE OF PESSIMISM)
33–36, 33 n.2, 43 n.19, 55–65

DIALOGUE OF PESSIMISM (see also
DIALOGUE BETWEEN A MASTER AND HIS
SERVANT) xii, xiii, 33–36, 43,
56 nn.4, 5, 58 n.11,
59 n.14, 60 n.23

DIALOGUE BETWEEN ŠŪPÊ-AMĒLĪ AND HIS
FATHER (see WISDOM OF ŠŪPÊ-AMĒLĪ)

DISPUTATION BETWEEN THE POPLAR
AND THE E'RU TREE 15

ENMEDURANKI LEGEND ("THE SEED OF
KINGSHIP," FOSTER, Before the Muses,
376–80) 6, 15

ESARHADDON TEMPLE DEDICATION
PRAYERS
ARAB 2.702 71
ARAB 2.670 74

ETANA 22 n.3

FABLE OF THE FOX 22

FABLE OF THE POPLAR 22

GILGAMESH 5, 7, 15, 21–29, 33,
56 n.6, 60 n.20, 73–74,
101 n.42

HYMN TO THE SUN (see SHAMASH HYMN)

INSTRUCTIONS OF ŠŪPÊ-AMĒLĪ (see WISDOM
OF ŠŪPÊ-AMĒLĪ)

INSTRUCTIONS OF ŠUPÊ–AWILUM 5

LAWS OF HAMMURABI 25, 40, 73

LETTER OF MARDUK-ŠUM-UŠUR
SAA 10, 174 16

LUDLUL BĒL NĒMEQI
xii, xiii, 3, 8 n.17, 9,
10 n.21, 11, 13, 14, 18

MARDUK'S ADDRESS TO THE DEMONS
18 n.41

SENNACHERIB'S DESCRIPTION OF HIS
PALACE
ARAB 2.94 88 n.101

SHAMASH HYMN xii, 33–36

SIDU 22

ŠIMÛ MILKA (see WISDOM OF ŠŪPÊ–AMĒLĪ)

A SUFFERER'S SALVATION (FOSTER, Before
the Muses, 410–11) 8, 18

TIGLATH–PILESER DESCRIPTION OF PALACE
88

URUK LIST OF RULERS AND SAGES
6 n.12, 13, 15, 16

VERSE ACCOUNT OF NABONIDUS 16, 25

VISION OF THE UNDERWORLD   82

WISDOM OF ŠŪPÊ–AMĒLĪ   37–51

Egyptian

INSTRUCTION OF AMENEMHET   40 n.15

INSTRUCTION OF ANY
39 n.11, 40 n.15, 43

INSTRUCTION OF KAGEMNI   40 n.15

INSTRUCTION OF PTAHHOTEP   40 n,. 15

Greek

HOMER
Odyssey
1.104–10   85 n,87
2.116–22   85 n.87
7.81–132   75 n.45
7.109–11   85 n.87
19.148–56   85 n.87

AESCHYLUS
Prometheus Bound   83

PLATO
2 Epistulae
314c   27 n.18

BEROSSOS
5, 15, 16, 83

Qumran

4Q372   84 n.86
11Q5 6:11–14   84 n.86

Philo

MOSES
2.6 and 12   84 n.84

Josephus

ANTIQUITIES
3:123   180–87

Mishnah and Talmud

M. 'ABOT
2:7   103

B. ŠABB. 30b   61

Index of Modern Authors

Abusch, Tsvi, 11 n.23, 18 n.41
Albertz, Rainer, 78 n.54, 79 n.56
Albright, W. F., 64 n.41
Al-Rawi, N. H., 5 n.4, 8 n.17
Alster, Bendt, 4 n.2, 6 n.10, 37 n.1
Altman, Alexander, 64 n.41
Anderson, Hugh, 99 n.26
Arnaud, Daniel, 56 n.6
Assmann, A., 83 n.77
Averbeck, Richard, 69 n.10, 71 n.19, 87 n.99
Azize, Joseph, 38 n.8

Baasten, M. F. J., 105 n.45
Bahrani, Z., 33 n.2, 56 n.4
Barré, Michael, 33 n.3
Barucq, André, 78 n.54
Banks, Michaela, 105 n.46
Baumann, Gerlinde, 105 n.46
Beaulieu, Paul-Alain, xi, 1-19, 26 n.15
Beentjes, Pancratius C., 101 nn.34, 35
Bergman, Varda, 60 n.22
Bergson, Henri, 59 n.15
Black, Jeremy A., xiii n.6
Bloch-Smith, Elizabeth, 84 n.84
Bohlen, Reinhold, 100 n.31
Borger, Rykle, 26 n.15-17, 75 nn.39-43, 88 n.105
Bottéro, Jean, 13 n.28, 33 n.2, 56 n.5, 58 n.11, 59 n.14, 60 n.23
Brill, A. A., 60 n.16
Brown, William P., 76 n.48
Buccellati, Giorgio, 37 n.2
Bunimovitz, Shlomo, 68 n.5
Burkert, Walter, 27 n.19
Burkes, Shannon, 99 n.28

Carigneaux, Antoine, 5 n.4
Carr, David, 102 n.39
Cazelles, Henri, 75 n.42
Charpin, Dominique, 69 n.8
Charlesworth, James, 100 n.30
Chavalas, Mark, 69 n.10
Civil, Miguel, 39 n.10, 70 n.18
Clifford, Richard J., xi-xiii, 67 n.1, 72 n.23, 75 n.42, 77 n.52, 78 n.54, 79 nn.58, 59, 83 n.77, 85 n.86, 86 n.93
Cohen, Mark E., 39 n.10
Cole, Stevan W., 17
Collins, John J., 77 n.52, 97 n.20, 101 n.36
Collon, Dominique 70 n.14
Cooper, Jerrold S., xiii n.5
Crenshaw, James, 58 n.12, 63 n.39, 64 n.43, 93-105
Critchley, Simon, 59 n.15, 60 n.17
Cross, Frank Moore, 89 n.106
Cunningham, G., xiii n.6

Day, John, xi, 38 n.6, 56 n.4
Diesel, A. A., 105 n.46
Delitzsch, Franz, 78 n.54
Doll, Peter, 77 n.52, 78 n.54, 79 nn.55, 56
del Olmo Lete, G., 73 n.30
de Moor, Johannes C., 38 n.7, 99 n.25
Demsky, Aaron, 56 n.6
Dever, William G., 68 n.5
de Savignac, Jean, 64 n.41
De Vries, Simon, 87 n.96
Dhorme, E., 70 n.17, 95 n.6
Dietrich, Manfred, 38 n.7, 40, 41, 56 n.6, 68 n.4
Di Lella, Alexander, 102 n.38

Dion, Paul-E., 68 n.8
Duesberg, Hilaire, 86 n.92
Dundes, Alan, 79 n.61

Ebeling, J., xiii, 33 n.4
Edzard, Dietz Ottto, xii, 8 n.17, 69 n.8
Ego, Beate, 67 n.2, 83 n.82
Eliade, Mircea, 70 n.15, 81 nn.65, 66
Ellis, Richard, 82 nn.71, 72
Emerton, J. A., xi n.l, 56 n.4
Epstein, Isadore, 76 n.49

Faust, Avraham, 68 n.5
Finkel, Irving, 12 nn. 27, 18, 13 n.31, 22
    n.5
Finkelstein, J. J., 33 n.4, 55 n.2
Fisher, Loren, 38 n.4
Fontaine, Carol R., 85 n.87
Forti, Tova, 38 n.7
Foster, Benjamin, xiii, 7 n.12, 8 n.13, 34
    nn.6, 7, 35 n.10, 38 nn. 5, 9, 55
    nn.1, 2, 60 n.20
Fox, Michael V., 38, 57 n.7, 58 n.12, 61
    n.24, 62 nn.28, 29, 31, 32, 78 nn.53,
    54, 79 nn.57, 58, 83 n.80, 86 n.9, 93
    n.1
Flückiger-Hawker, E., xiii n.6
Frame, Grant, 6 n.11,13 nn.29, 30
Frankfort, Henri, 72 n.23
Fransen, I., 86 n.92
Freedman, Harry, 76 n.49
Freud, Sigmund, 60 nn.16, 18

Gadamer, Hans-G., 81 n.68
Gaher, Hans D., 44 n.20
Gammie, John G., 73 n.29
Garelli, Paul, 6 n.11
Geller, Mark J., 12 n.28
George, Andrew, 5 nn.4, 5, 6, 7; 8 n.17,
    12 n.28, 21 n.1, 23 nn.8, 10, 24 n.11
Gesche, Petra, 10 n.21, 14 n.33
Gianto, Augustinus, 38 n.8
Gilbert, Maurice, 104 n.4
Ginsberg, H. L., 61 n.26, 64 n.41
Gitin, Seymour, 68 n.5
Goatly, Andrew, 72 n.28
Good, Edwin M., 62 n.33

Gordis, Robert, 62 n.27
Gordon, Edmund, 37 n.l
Grayson, A. K., 15 n.37, 71 n.19, 74
    nn.34, 36, 74 nn.34-37
Greenberg, Moshe, 33 n.4, 55 n.2
Greenfield, Jonas C., 75 n.42, 93 n.1
Greenspahn, Frederick, 57 n.10
Greenstein, Edward L., 33 n.2, 43 n.19,
    55-65
Gressmann, Hugo, xii

Harm, Robert, 67 n.2
Hakham, Amos, 98 n.23
Hallo, William W., xiii, 7 n.12, 8 n.13, 64
    n.41
Harvey, John E., 98 n.24
Heeßel, Nils P., 10 n.22
Hengel, Martin, 100 n.31
Höffken, Peter, 104 n.43
Holloway, Stephen W., 68 n.4
Horstmanshoff, H. F. J., 10 n.21
Horowitz, Wayne, 69 n.13
Houtman, Cornelius, 84, 85 n.89
Hübner, Ulrich, 97 n.21
Huffman, Herbert, 76 n.48
Hurowitz, Victor Avigdor, xi, 33-51, 71
    nn.19, 20, 22, 72 n.24, 76 n.47, 87
    n.98, 76 n.47, 87 n.98
Hurvitz, Avi, 105 n.45
Hunger, Hermann, 12 nn.24, 25, 26 n.16

Jacobsen, Thorkild, 5 n.3, 68 n.3
Janowski, Bernd, 67 n.2, 83 n.82
Japhet, Sara, 61 n.26
Johnson, Mark, 72 n.28
Jones, Bruce J., 64 n.41

Kaiser, Otto, 100 n.31
Kämmerer, Thomas R., 38 n.7
Kaydana, Götz, 38 n.7
Keel, Othmar, 67 n.2, 72 n.26, 77 n.50
Khanjian, John, 38 n.4, 56 n.6
Kienast, Burkhart, 22 n.4
King, Philip J., 84 n.84
Klein, Jacob, 8 n.14, 72 n.25
Knauf, Ernst Axel, 97 n.21
Knierim, Rolf, 81 n.66
Knight, Douglas A., 97 n.21

Kolarcik, Michael, 100 n.33
Kramer, S. N., 64 n.41, 69 n.11, 85 n.87
Krüger, Annette, 83 n.82
Kuhrt, Amélie, 68 n.2
Kutsko, John F., 104 n.4

Laato, Antti, 99 n.23
Lakoff, George, 72 n.28
Lambert, W. G., xii, 3 n.1, 6 n.11, 8
    nn.15, 18, 9 nn.19, 20, 12 nn.26, 28,
    14 n.33, 15 n.35, 18 n.41, 21 n.2, 22
    n.6, 35 n.10, 37 n.1, 38 n.6; 42 n.18,
    43 n.19, 56 n.4, 70 n.18
Launderville, Dale, 81 n.64
Langdon, Stephen, 22 n.7
Leuchter, Mark, 98 n.24
Levenson, Jon D., 76 n.48, 81 n.66, 84
    n.84
Levine, Baruch, 68 n.5
Levine, Etan, 62 n.34
Lichtheim, Miriam, 39 n.11, 40 n.15
Liebermann, Stephen J., 37 n.1
Livingstone, Alasdair, 70 n.16, 82 n.72
Loader, J. A., 62 n.27
Lohfink, Norbert, 104 n.44, 105 n.45
Long, Burke O., 87 n.97
Longman, Tremper, 64 n.41
Luckenbill, D. D., 88 n.104
Lundquist, John, 76 n.48

Machinist, Peter, xi, 67 n.1, 74 n.37, 91
    n.1
Maier, John, 69 n.11, 85 n.87
Malik, Charles, 81 n.70
Mattila, S. L., 100 n.31
Mattingly, Gerald, 8 n. 13
Maul, Stefan M., 11 n.23
McBride, S. Dean, 76 n.48, 84 n.83
McKane, William, 44 n.21
Mendenhall, George, 76 n.48
Meyer, Werner, 7 n.12
Millard, A. R., 70 n.18
Moran, William L., 23 n.9
Morris, Sarah P., 67 n.2, 75 n.46
Muraoka, T., 105 n.45
Murphy, Roland E., 33 n.3, 77 n.52, 78
    n.54, 97 n.21, 99 n.27

Newsom, Carol, 79 n.61, 95 n.6
Noth, Martin, 85 n.88, 87 n.95
Nougayrol, Jean, 8 nn.15, 16, 38 n.3
Novák, Mirko, 71 n.77

Packer, J. L., 77 n.51
Pardee, Dennis, 79 n.60, 83 n.7
Paris, P. J., 97 n.21
Parpola, Simo, 16 n.38, 60 n.20, 71 n.22,
    74 n.32
Paul, Shalom, 95 n.12, 97 n.17
Paulos, John A., 60 n.18
Peckham, Brian, 98 n.24
Perdue, Leo G., 72 n.28, 73 n.29
Plöger, Otto, 78 n.54
Pritchard, James B., xiii

Rad, Gerhard von, 79 n.59, 81 n.69, 93
    n.2
Reiner, Erica, 8 n.15
Ringgren, Helmer, 60 n.21, 78 n.54
Robson, I., xiii n.6
Röllig, Wolfgang, 22 n.3
Römer, Willem H. Ph., xiii, 37 n.1
Roth, Martha, 73 n.31
Russell, John M., 88 n.100

Salters, Robert B., 61 n.26
Samet, Nili, 33 n.4
Sanmartin, J., 73 n.30
Sauer, Georg 101 n.35
Schaudig, Hans-Peter, 16 n.39
Schafer, Aaron, 64 n.41
Schellenberg, Annette, 93 n.1
Schloen, J. David, 68 nn.5, 6, 68 n.9, 81
    n.67
Schmid, Hans Heinrich, 99 n.27
Schoors, Antoon, 38 n.8
Schniedewind, William M., 69 n.8
Scott, R. B. Y., 64 n.42
Schwienhorst-Schönberger, L., 100 n.31,
    104 n.44
Sheppard, Gerald T., 77 n.51
Seminara, Stefano, 38 n.7, 41
Seow, Choon-Leong, 63 n.40, 75 n.44
Seux, M.-J., 34
Sjöberg, Åke, 37 n.1

Skehan, Patrick W., 102 n.37
Smith, Duane, 38 n.4
Smith, Mark S., 67 n.1, 68 n.5, 83 n.79
Snell, Daniel, 79 n.60
Soderland, S. K., 77 n.51
Soskice, Janet M., 81 n.64
Sparks, Kenton, xiii, n.7, 67 n.1
Speiser, E. A., 33 n.4, 35 n.9, 55 n.2, 58 n.13, 59
Stager, Lawrence E., 68 n.5
Stol, Marten, 10 n.22, 68 n.8
Stolz, E., 98 n.22
Streck, Maximilian, 70 n.16
Sukenik, E. L., 64 n.41
Sweet, Ronald F. G., 25 n.14, 73 n.29, 82 n.75

Tadmor, Hayim, 68 n.7, 88 n.102
Taylor, J., xiii n.6
Terrien, Samuel, 96 n.13, 97 n.18
Toy, Crawford H., 78 n.54
Trask, Willard R., 70 n.15

Van Buren, E. D., 74 n.38, 82 n.75
VanderKam, James C., 97 n.19
van der Ploeg, J., 78 n.54
van der Toorn, Karel, xi, 11 n.23, 21-29, 97 n.21
Van De Mieroop, Marc, 33 n.2, 56 n.4
Van Dijk, Jacobus, 6 n.12
van Hecke, Pierre, 72 n.28
Van Leeuwen, Raymond, 33 n.3, 67-89, 97 n.21
Van Peursen, W. Th., 105 n.45

Verbrugghe, Gerald P., 5 n.8
von Soden, Wolfram, xiii, 34 n.5, 37 n.1, 38 n.4
Vollmer, J., 94 n.5

Waltke, Bruce K., 77 n.51
Wassermann, Nathan, 33 n.4
Watson, Wilfred G. E., 38 n.7
Weippert, Manfred, 28 n.20, 97 n.21
Weisman, Ze'ev, 55 n.1, 62 n.35
Weiss, Meir, 62 n.37
Wenham, Gordon, 76 n.46
West, Martin L., 67 n.2, 75 n.45
Westermann, Claus, 79
Whybray, R. Norman, 78 n.54, 79 n.57, 86 n.90, 87
Whiting, Robert M., 71 n.22
Wicke-Reuler, U., 100 n.31
Wickersham, John M., 5 n.8
Wilcke, Claus, 37 n.1, 83 n.77
Willis, John T., 100 n.29
Wilson, J. V. Kinder, 22 n.3
Winston, David, 100 n.31
Winter, Irene, 74 n.37
Wischmeyer, Oda, 103 n.41
Wiseman, D. J., 8 n.17, 68 n.4, 72 n.23, 74 n.36
Wood, Joyce Rilett, 98 n.24

Yellin, David, 62 n.36
Younger, K. Lawson, 69 n.10

Zer-Kavod, Mordechai, 61 nn.24, 25
Zólyomi, G., xiii n.6

Lightning Source UK Ltd.
Milton Keynes UK
UKOW051948040412

190187UK00001B/42/A